CH00840109

The Circle
&
The Sword

To Scott

Nigel Mortimer

Thank you for all your support & FCD mate,

Best Wishes

Nigel 2023

WISDOM BOOKS

Also available as an Ancient Booklet – eBook
Ancient Mail Verlag Werner Betz
www.ancientmail.de

Nigel Mortimer

First published in Great Britain in 2013 by Wisdom Books
This edition published in 2013 by Wisdom Books

Copyright c.2014 by Nigel Mortimer
The moral right of the author has been asserted
All rights reserved.

ISBN-13: 9781500803292

ISBN-10: 1500803294

No part of this publication may be reproduced, stored in a retrieval system, or transmitted in any form or by any means, without the prior permission in writing of the publisher, nor be otherwise circulated in any form of binding or cover other than that in which it is published and without a similar condition including this condition being imposed on the subsequent purchases.

Typeset in Garamond by M Rules
Wisdom Books
A division of House of Books Yorkshire
Sutcliffe Buildings
Settle
North Yorkshire
England BD24 9EZ

The Circle & The Sword

The Cow & Claf Rocks, Ilkley Moor -the face of a sleeping giant is said to haunt the larger 'Cow' rock face.

An ancient tumulus mound behind White Wells

Nigel Mortimer

PREFACE

This is a true story.

In our modern age, it it remains hard to envisage a God who would continue to communicate with mankind through visions. But what if it had always been that way, and there had always been visionary communion between something which we call God, and the race of beings we call Humans. Could it be true that we have distanced ourselves from our creator, and in doing so, we have lost through time, the ability to acknowledge that which is there before our very eyes? If God is all around us, then maybe there are really those, who being aware, literally do see the light.

In a small Yorkshire town, on the edge of one of England's most famous landmarks, Ilkley Moor, something amazing took place during the summer months of 1994. A vision of a fantastic golden double- edged sword appeared to the congregation of Ilkley's Parish Church. At the very same time, an identical sword was seen in a vision at an ancient stone circle on the adjacent moorland. Both places had religious and paranormal connections, were steeped in myth, legend and folklore, and became the focus for sightings of UFOs & strange and mysterious balls of light.
In both cases, those involved in these extraordinary revelations, pronounced that God had spoken to them and through this enlightenment, soon became aware that this was the beginning of the return to Earth of the Celestials; angelic beings existing between mankind and his creator.

ACKNOWLEDGMENTS

This book is dedicated to everyone who finds truth within themselves, finds courage to question all, and finds compassion to share their love. Sincere thanks goes out to the following people, in appreciation of their help and support:

Jon Hurst & Jan Jackman -like a brother and sister to me, and much more., Helju Bland - for first initiating my communion with the Celestials., the late David Barclay – a pioneer of fringe ufology, a man ahead of his time., Jenny Randles - the first to listen when the OBOL struck, Steve Hart, Martin Daglass, and the crew of the IUN - nostalgic days investigating together all things weird and wonderful. , Marie Campbell – for making me aware of the Land of the Dragon.,

Loving wishes go to Sara & Ben, Lee & Warren, wonderful children now grown up, my sisters, Lynda, Sharon, Debbie and their families, and to my Mum Lilly - loving thanks for sitting up half the nights with me looking for UFOs in those open starry skies.....another, also way ahead of her time. Helen, a seeker of Angels: she 'knew' the true meaning of the 'curly whirly' spirals and touched my heart with her love when others failed to see the truth.

Also my loving thanks and appreciation goes to those soul aspects long departed, who worked alongside me, silently and unseen, in my quest for the truth: Akhenaten & his daughter Scota, Hakon the Good, and the living essence of truth and wisdom, Sharlek, without who's guidance this book would never have been completed. Thanks to Daniela Mattes for her help in updating this book. A special friend from the distant past, and an inspiration in the present day, a name to be remembered when the future arrives. My apologies to anyone else not mentioned here, my thoughts are with you with no lesser degree of appreciation. Thank you all.

CONTENTS

CHAPTER ONE

THE CALL OF BACKSTONES

Ilkley Moor is probably one of Yorkshire's most famous landmarks and tourist attractions, being visited by thousands of people every summer. As its gentle grassy slopes rise to rocky summits, a panoramic scenario unfolds over the Wharfe Valley below. To most, Ilkley Moor is a picture-postcard setting, but at times, it can take on an utterly opposite nature, evoking a strange sense of loneliness and desolation. At these times, the moor reveals a hidden and darker side, one acknowledged in the late Victorian era, as the 'Haunted Moor'...

At the turn of the century, the moor became known as a place not to be ventured onto during the late hours. They named it the 'place of horrors', due to the many strange, inexplicable occurrences of a paranormal nature; involving unusual nocturnal lights, phantom-like entities, and ghostly sensations which manifested at megalithic ancient sites. In modern times, we tend to account for these occurrences with up-to-date connotations, the lights become UFOs, and the phantoms become their Alien occupants.

The phenomena behind these, seem to be from a comparable source and can be found to occur at the same locations on the moor, playing out some kind of hidden mystery on any unsuspecting witness? There seems to be a purpose behind this, there seems to be a reason, but just what that is, promotes a mystery in itself.

During the 1980's, along with a team of paranormal researchers, I began to examine this hidden history alongside the on-going reports of UFO's at Ilkley Moor. Little did I know at that time, how that involvement would change my life, so dramatically that it would become a life-long quest to search out the truth behind Ilkley Moor's elusive mystery. Something up there on those moors was calling out to be recognised, something that had been a part of the region for a very long time, something that could never be ignored.

On the morning of Saturday 15th July, 1989, the midsummer sun began to rise and spread a golden glow across Wharfedale. All was so peaceful, and the scenery quite breathtaking; such was the view that opened up before my eyes as I made my way down towards the town of Ilkley after an uneasy night spent out on the moor.

I had spent the evening with friends, Paul Bennett and Andy Tyson, who themselves had been witness to what we called the 'Ilkley thing'. This was a rare stay out on the moors for me, being a busy working father of a young family at the time, I found chances to venture out onto the moors, opportunities that were few and far between. The time was now 2.45am, a swirling mist enveloped my casual trainers, treading ground that began its own long journey to warm up. The previous night had been for me, one with an intense coldness that I felt within me, yet in contradiction of the summertime weather conditions that were apparent to all.

Puzzled, I reflected on how my two friends had continued to sleep through this strange coldness, and I continued to make my way down and off that unwelcoming moor. I sat down, after slipping and sliding over slabs of glass-like rock and dew-laden grasses. My casual trainers were no match for that terrain, and I wished that I had wore boots to assist this tricky descent. As I looked up, I caught a movement of something in the skies to the north; an orange-red colored ball of intense light, comparable to the size of the sun. I knew, it was not the sun –the Sun does not move at speed across the sky. This pseudo sun came to a sudden stop, it rested, silent, motionless at a position which would be somewhere near to where I lived in the village of Addingham, about 3 miles from my position on the edge of the moor. Whatever I had seen, it was not there when I reached home, exhausted from the long trek and ever reoccurring thoughts of why such an uneasy night's ordeal. Back at home and in the comfort of my bed , it wasn't long before I began to drift off into sleep. How I longed for the safe and comforting arms of my wife, who was still out working as a night-nurse at Ilkleys' geriatric hospital. I was alone at home in my 'unusual' interest.

Susan, not surprisingly, had a caring heart for the peoples of this world, with little need to find herself exploring matters of the unexplained. My two beautiful children were far too young to know anything about their father's obsession, as far as I was concerned at that time. What! There father believing in UFOs and the like! No, I was a normal bloke, with a normal family and a normal job. Why should they suffer the ridicule that so often accompanies these things? If I saw UFOs, then that was my concern, and there was no need to convert anyone to believe in something which even I had to admit, was nothing more than a mystery remaining in the realms of obscurity at the very best. That is why I would hide all my books on the subject - kept under lock and key in the highest cupboard. This was my quest, this was something that had effected me, and I would journey alone to seek out an answer to it all. Talk about being lonely in ones work...you don't know the half of it.

I never knew if I was actually dreaming when I started to think back over the events that had led me up to my visit onto Ilkley Moor. How it all had started for me, back in November 1980, then an office clerk in my home town of Otley. That's when I first became aware of the orange balls of lights - UFOs that were being reported all over the Wharfe Valley. My life was typical at that time, of a spirited teenager in his first job, working the week to look forwards to the weekends, when I would ride my motorcycle with friends around the Yorkshire Dales, and maybe take in the odd pint or two down at the local pub. In the early hours of November 30th all of that changed for good.

In the week prior to the experience, odd things began to happen in and around me, which became more than pure coincidental. There seemed to be an unusual atmosphere of kinds within the house, as if there was someone there, unseen, occupying its rooms. Loud banging noises, which carried their own energy, were heard by my sisters and my mother; on one occasion her bedroom door being literally flung open with the force of this sudden intrusion! A most bizarre event took place, when my sister's hair, unbeknown to her at the time, had been re-styled by invisible hands in the middle of the night whilst she had been sleeping.

All of this strange poltergeist-like activity continued until the morning I saw the OBOL. I awoke, for no apparent reason, in the early hours. Outside the house, a shroud of darkness still covered the adjacent fields that ran northwards out towards the top-secret establishment at Menwith Hill.

The skies above, were crystal clear, crisply bright with an icy coldness. My half-open gaze wandered across the heavens. Did I see that certain small star begin to move?

I initially put it down to my imagination, or maybe still a continuing dream. I looked again, and let my hand move out onto the damp window- ledge. That small star, was moving! Within split-seconds it became larger and much more defined, it seemed to be hurtling with a tremendous speed right in my direction. Moments passed by, then, hanging motionless a spherical object, stationary, and in line with my eyesight, it became the only importance in a situation where every sound, sensation and awareness of reality became void. All the time I watched in awe, I kept telling myself that I shouldn't be seeing this, I was not supposed to be seeing this.....it was almost as if the object had an air of dignity about it, and I felt that I was not worthy, indeed no person was worthy, of laying human eyes on this majestic sight.

But, how could this be so? I wasn't looking at a person. It was a 'thing' of the skies, an animated object without a life of its' own. Or was it? I began to work out in my mind that whatever it was, it was more like a vision, than anything else. Not that I had seen a vision before mind you, yet its presence secured itself within me, in a way that I will never forget. As the OBOL hovered at about 50 feet from the ground, and less than 200 meters away, I felt myself being charged with an ecstatic sensation; an awareness that I was a part of the whole environment around me, that all life was precious, and that there was great importance in what I was experiencing. And, with that, moving towards East Wood, the UFO made its silent and ghostly departure.

As it did so, my heart seemed to be pulled physically out of my body, my emotions erupting with the sense of ages of human passion and hurt, overbearing, and leaving me a shell, empty, and lacking that which had been with me before this communion with the unknown, a sense of knowing who I was.

When I woke up later in the morning, I had no recollection of the experience. Even if it had been no more than a dream, then I still had no remembrance of it at all, yet, inwardly, as I prepared to get ready for work, I felt that I had not had a good nights sleep and that something had awoken me in the night, but I did not know what. At work, I bumped into Yvette, the switchboard operator and a pleasant friend, who I would spend some time each morning chatting to over our coffee break. This morning, our conversation turned to the events of the weekend and what each of us had been doing. Unknowingly, Yvette began to utter these words, " My mother saw something really unusual in the sky last night", I listened with a wry smile on my face, with hidden thoughts concerning a sweet old lady mistaking some nocturnal celestial event, but remained silent as she continued,

"It was like an orange colored ball, about the size of the full-moon, which fizzed and crackled with energy...

She went on, "Did you hear about it Nigel? She saw it over East Woods, near to where you live....."

Later, I was to learn that Yvette's mother had seen the

same UFO, at the same time (actually 1.00am), and at the same location (she lived at Burley In Wharfedale, only a few miles from my home.) and in the years to come, I discovered that others had been witness to the same experience in November, 1980. All of the day at work, something puzzled me. Why wouldn't the thoughts of Yvette's story leave my mind, pressing me to listen to its inner voice , with very little chance of being able to forget her story, even though any possibility that it could have been a real event was remote in the very least as far as I was concerned.

Tea-time arrived after work, then I retired to my bedroom. All seemed normal there, all in order, apart from the newsprint that ran across the top of the local newspaper for that day, 'Police chase UFO'. Yvette's story had made the headlines.

I looked up at the window sill, then back down at the newspaper. Something caught my eye, a glint of sunlight reflecting off an ornament which was 'out of place'. I had moved it during the experience, and with that sudden realisation, the whole of my own involvement became apparent once more. The action instigated by whatever lay at the heart of this, then the truth, had been revealed by some kind of trigger, and like a video-recorder on rewind, I once more, lived through an episode that would change my life's course.

In order to try make sense of all the reports of OBOLs I came across after 1980, involving accounts from all over the world, an obsession overtook me and the only thing of importance above all else, was a quest to reveal what lay behind the UFO enigma? One thing I was absolutely certain about, was that this phenomenon was very real, it existed, and normal people were interacting with it! They weren't just seeing strange lights in the skies, but they were also undergoing some kind of what we might call a spiritual awakening; a communion between the phenomenon and ourselves.

I was to see the OBOL again in 1981, but not in our current place and time. I had been lazily reading a book about crystal gazing –this was to be a path I took after the OBOL experience of the year before, becoming increasingly interested in all aspects of the paranormal and psychic abilities. Soon, I was practicing with a crystal of my own. I gazed into the quartz deeply, letting my thoughts wander. After a time, a greenish mist enveloped the crystal sphere that I held in my hand. A faint lighted area drew my attention, and searching deeper within its realms of uncertainty, not knowing what I might just find there? A second later, the light dispersed. I was left peering into a scene that opened up before me; somewhere from the distant past, somewhere very ancient.

I was looking down from atop a huge stone structure being constructed out of giant blocks of granite. I looked out across the panoramic landscape firmly fixed in my mind's eye, and I knew in that moment that I was in the middle of a river-edged desert. I had been transported back in time, back to the days of who we call today, the Ancient Egyptians. I was then standing upon a long ramp that climbed up the side of a building. At my side, someone else, a female stood holding my hand in hers. I tried to look around at her face, but wasn't 'allowed' to, but I could see that she was wearing a fine and beautiful garment that flowed in a slight breeze. Her hair was short, black and wavy. This woman was important. She overlooked the work that was being undertaken by others, small figures that moved the stones with casual ease. She moved her arm across in front of me and with it, I heard a loud droning noise. Incredibly, stones that weighed tons, moved off the ground and settled on one another as light as feathers! She raised her arm skywards and pointed an elegant finger to the heavens, and as she did this, I seemed to be there, in the clear blue sky above. In front of my gaze, miles high, I watched in amazement, as an orange colored disc, spinning at immense speed, very much like the Sun, but, different in its' own way.

Shortly after that experience I began to feel elevated spiritually. Within a year I had not only seen something that proved to me that the OBOLs were something real, yet apart from humanity in their realness. They seemed to have a personality, they seemed to be alive, and they seemed to 'know' me. In a way, I would say I was under the impression that the phenomena was more aware of who I was, than I was of myself. I felt humbled and began to see that I was significantly small in the whole scheme of things. At that time I would not have considered it to have been anything spiritual at all, but there were, upon reflection, overtones of an illuminating and life changing event, which I suppose could parallel what some would call a spiritual awakening. I kept having psychic experiences and seeing UFOs on and off throughout the 1980s, so much so, that I began to find within myself some kind of realisation that maybe I had been 'selected' by whatever lay at the heart of the phenomenon. The more that I sought the truth, more and more 'evidence' became apparent to me, and it seemed too coincidental that it should arrive just when I would need it to help further my inquiries. But, there was a problem here. What does one do, when all one can think, live and breath something that seems to have no conclusive ending? Although I didn't realise it at that time, my obsession was taking over my life, and unwittingly, I was putting just as important things, like my wife and beautiful young family on hold. A recipe for matrimonial disaster. How can anyone justify the sudden and compelling urgency to leave the house in the middle of dinner, because inwardly 'the call' to be at a certain location, without question, had to be followed. That was my curse back then, but I had been privy to something that far outweighed the consequences, and I knew my

Above: Backstones Circle viewed from the western sheepfold.

actions would eventually push those I loved away from me. It was like a drug. I couldn't get enough of 'them' - I was on my own quest for the truth and quite selfishly, right or wrong, nothing else mattered.

The night out on Ilkley Moor had been at the instigation of Paul Bennett, a Bradford born Earth Mysteries enthusiast and good friend back then, who had asked me for some help in locating a 'lost' stone circle. He knew about the psychic awareness that had been growing in me since my encounter with the OBOL in 1980. Now, some nine years on, it seemed right for me to listen to this voice within, and follow what psychically I knew to be right. I used a form of dowsing in order to reveal information that we would not be able to locate with our normal senses.Backstone Circle had been known to the Victorians, but at the turn of the last century, when farming and domestic clearing of the moorlands destroyed many ancient sites, the actual location became lost to memory and local historical record. If we were to be able to locate the site, we knew that we would succeed where archaeologists' had failed, for the past one hundred years, and that would be an achievement in itself, but again, inwardly I was certain that there lay a higher importance behind all of this. The quest was on.

'There was a rude circle of rocks on the reach behind the old white wells fifty years ago, tumbled into such a confusion that you had to look once and then again, before you saw what lay under your eyes; the stones were very large and there was no trace of line about them, and this may have been a rude outpost of the tribe for the defense of the great living spring and also of Llecan (Ilkley) lying below.' Rev. Robert Collier, 1885.
Where does one start trying to locate a needle in a

haystack? That was the task ahead, and most sensible folk would give up before they even got started. But, something else was driving this forward, maybe it was a test to see how far I would go, or possibly a wild goose chase. We were talking about an area of Ilkley Moor that stretched across six square miles of remote landscape, undulating and pitted with hollows and ravines overgrown with four foot high bracken.

I will never forget the sense of utter amazement I felt as I rounded the corner on the moorland trackway adjacent to the well-known stone called the tree-of-life, next to Backstone Beck. An energy filled the air, an expectation, unseen but felt with the certainty of centuries, I trod on forwards towards my holy grail. Echoing the words of Rev. Collier, I had to look once and then again, the second time making no mistake with two large standing stones in situ on the outer-circumference remains of a double ring stone circle.

Excited, and fisting the air in triumph, I beheld that which lay out in front of me. No wonder it had been lost to time, for farmers had built walling in amongst the stones, and a sheep-fold dissected this ancient site into two halves. I took time to pull back at the overgrown bracken, frantically trying to trace the outline of the circle. I felt in awe of the site, as if I was entering some great lost cathedral, so in reverence, I closed my eyes and gave my own thanks to God and thinking that whatever had led me to this place, would surely understand this faith within man.

It was now mid-morning, the following day from my uneasy night out at the newly re-discovered Backstone Circle. I had been sleeping in bed for several hours and upon wakening, I heard the voice of Susan as she left the house to go out shopping. Closing the garden gate, I heard another voice, this one excited and at the same time, somewhat agitated. In urgent conversation, I heard someone say,

"My mother was woken up in the early hours of this morning at about 3.30am, after hearing a loud droning noise....did you hear it too? I got up myself to see what all the commotion was, and I couldn't believe what I was looking at! It was a large oval object with loads of smaller lights that gave-off a strange orange red glow that flooded down onto your rooftop. It was no aircraft I've ever seen before, I'm sure of that, he went on, "whatever it was, it moved away as soon as I looked at it, towards Beamsley Beacon, (north-west of Addingham) and suddenly there was no sound coming from it. All was very quiet indeed."

Seemingly, this was the same OBOL that I had observed on my way down from the moors earlier that morning, but what was it now doing over my very rooftop. My wife listened with half-interest, quickly making her excuse to catch the bus, and obviously putting any talk of UFOs and such things to the back of her mind for the rest of the day, probably the safest place for such things in an uncertain mind? No, she would wait until later, when she could talk to me about it and try to rationalise an answer to this madness. By then, our children would be safe in bed and out of earshot too. Susan not wanting them to be worried that ET had paid a visit to the Mortimer household.
But, the two children were holding secrets of their own, and both Susan and I had no idea just how involved they

were already in what had occurred whilst I had been out at Backstone Circle. Sara, then our five year old daughter awoke from her sleep a little earlier at 3.15 am, she opened her eyes and jumped with a start! Looking through the half opened bedroom door, she found it difficult to keep her eyes open, as if she was being forced to slip back into the slumber of sleep. Raising her hand to cover her face and peeping through protective fingers, Sara stared at the ghostly humanoid figure that was ascending the stairs, reaching the top and then vanishing into thin air! The heavy sleepiness finally overcame her, and she gave in.

Susan returned home and we all had tea together. The children kept quiet, and Sara was as normal as ever. For the sake of the children, we had decided to put the whole experience behind us, for it seemed that this thing was becoming too close for comfort, and the last I wanted was to impose my 'obsession' onto the innocence of youth. This was made difficult, in that the local press had run a front-page piece describing reports of the UFO being seen by a number of other people up and down the Wharfe Valley around the time of our own experiences. One of these had been seen within fifteen minutes of my own sighting of the OBOL as I came down off the moor. It must have been the same object I had seen, and no matter how we tried to turn away from it, the family found itself the focus of something which became increasingly intrusive.

The following night at about 19.00 hrs, Sara was back in her bed again. As if to play out some kind of repeat sequence, events began to unfold once more, and silently, the darkened figure appeared at the top of the stairs, less than nine feet from her bedroom. Expecting it to vanish as before, she fought with her senses as the form floated just above the floor towards her, getting closer, close enough to see that this entity was a female. Now, she got the impression that the first had been a male, due to the stern looking features compared to this more elegant apparition. Both had been wearing what she took to be a tight-fitting, black, one -piece diving suit, a cowled hood over the head and the whole of the face exposed.

Researcher Paul Bennett discusses the rediscovery of the lost stone circle.

The end of 1989 became increasingly difficult for all of the family. We knew that we shared something, an awareness of things that should not take place, so we tried to ignore this, but it just would not go away. Sara and her brother Ben were seeing figures in the house that would mimic the looks, and movements of Susan and myself; on one occasion Sara watched as one impersonator of her mother, dressed exactly the same as her, walked right through a wall unit in the living room, while Susan was busy working upstairs! We all felt that we were being watched, even when there was nobody physically there. The pressure became too much. My involvement was effecting my working life, and everyday chores became pointless to me. Shamefully, my family was becoming a poor second-best to the quest I had undertaken and Susan could see clearly how all of this had been effecting us all. I quit my job, and she divorced me within weeks. I had lost everything that I loved in my life, and now found myself alone in a world in which the UFO-nut makes very few understanding friends.

Alien Contact

The balls of lights phenomenon (BOLs) date back many centuries. People were observing these kinds of UFO before any kind of writing as communication had even evolved on this planet. More recently, the same kind of phenomena continues to be reported alongside other types of UFO experiences. Are they all linked together, or should we examine these BOLs in a completely separate way to other UFO experiences? When the late David Barclay encountered a large orange sphere that was only feet away from where he stood outside his home in Shipley, West Yorkshire, he got the very real impression that 'it' was observing him. He felt that he was being 'followed by a stranger'. Others have described something similar, some witnesses are very frightened, yet others feel secure -inwardly knowing that whatever they are gazing upon, it seems to mean them no harm. These feelings are very apparent during the experience and throughout the observation, as if the witness is meant to acknowledge

Orange Ball Of Light above Morris Dancers, photographed at Appletreewick 1983
Copyright: N.Mortimer /CONNECT 1983.

them and take note of how they are feeling. Many reports indicate that in particular with OBOL sightings, there is this strange, almost personal interaction, something that would suggest that rather than the UFO being an object, it acts and causes a reaction we would associate with an encounter with another person. In 1981, around the Wharfe Valley region, not many miles from where David Barclay had his encounter, another witness to this phenomenon Steve Hart, was traveling home on public transport. Close to Addingham, he noticed hanging in the sky over the local moorlands, a large orange ball of light. Suddenly, as he watched it, an intense feeling of sorrow and dread overcame him which lasted as long as he had the object in sight. When Steve later arrived home in Leeds, he was devastated to learn that his grandmother had just passed away. She had died at the same time that he had been watching the OBOL some hours earlier. Maybe this phenomena has the ability to see what lay in our immediate futures, maybe it is some kind of signal or sign or premonition? Whatever they are, OBOLs are real enough to have been photographed and caught on video film too. The encounter that Steve Hart had, and its associate 'coincidence' of his grandmother's death at the time of the experience, is puzzling. What is even more amazing is that this very same thing happened again, at almost the same location, and this time the OBOL was caught on film.

The photograph opposite page, was taken by the owner of a public house in Appletreewick, North Yorkshire, on mid-summer's day in 1983. Although she did not see the OBOL at the time, when the film was developed she noticed the large sphere, located behind tree branches only yards away. The Morris Dancers too, were totally unaware of this invisible visitor, yet later a strange story was to unfold.
The West Yorkshire UFO Research Group conducted an investigation later that year into this photographic case, involving Kodak. After an extensive study, they proclaimed that 'whatever the object was (and it could have been several things), it was there when the photograph had been taken. You can see branches from the tree in the foreground, yet the OBOL covers part of the hillside behind it. Interestingly, directly below its

position, investigators found the site of an ancient well. Some local campers in the locality, came forward with reports that they had seen strange orange lights in the sky, only days before.

Later that day, Simon Grey (pseudonym), the Morris dancer seen below the OBOL, headed home to Leeds. In a re-run of Steve Hart's experience, he too found bad news awaiting him there. He learned that at the very same time the photograph had been taken, his brother had suddenly died of a heart attack. It would seem that these OBOLs are aware of our human affairs. Maybe they know what is about to happen and have the ability to tune-in to our human feelings.

On the far side of Leeds, some fifteen miles from Ilkley Moor, medium Phil Hine had received a message from the beyond,

"Something has been awoken, something that had been lain dormant for thousands of years, yet now could be found by any man on the moors above Ilkley."

He was told in his message that a newly found stone circle was a gateway, a link between this world and others, and those that used it, wished to enter into our world. Hine had no idea that Backstone Circle had just been rediscovered, or about the associated events that had unfolded at Addingham, but his words remained prophetic, even more-so, when in June 1991, Paul Bennett witnessed for himself strange apparitions that weaved their way around the upright stones at the circle site. Phantom figures with little form, appeared to be moving at speed between the stones of the outer circle, then becoming a spinning vortex of pure blue light, coning upwards into the skies above. Then, a week later, two teenage girls walked alongside Backstone Circle and were amazed to see an OBOL in broad daylight, this being the first of the recurring events to take place at this enigmatic and yet very ancient place.

I did a lot of wandering around those moors in the latter months of 1989. I was a lost man, without the love of my wife and separated from the children I loved dearly. I was heartbroken, and yet there always remained that inner sense which had been with me since 1980, that I was never alone. Call it an inner-strength, or maybe an awareness that there were presences around me, which although unseen, were there, guiding and orchestrating my life. If they were, then what happened next, must have been literally 'on the cards'.

Tree Of Life Stone, Ilkley Moor - ancient cup & ring carved rock.

Nigel Mortimer

Dowsing at White Wells

The Ilkley Parish Register for August 1793, records a singular accident to a young girl, little Ann Harper, aged nine years. She was drowned in one of the baths whilst attempting to bathe herself as far as is known. In 1982, the babysitter of the owners of the baths at White Wells, became terrified at the apparition she saw, a ghostly figure of a young girl weeping at the side of the icy cold pool.

In the works Upper Wharfedale, we learn that a curiously sculptured stone which is now actually a part of the flooring at Ilkley Parish Church, shows a half length human figure wearing some kind of skullcap. In each of its hands are held two serpent like rods in the upright position.

Most believe that this was a statue of the Roman Goddess Verbia, protector of rivers and waters. The author of the book, Harry Speight, draws the inference that 'the two

28

separate serpent objects are intended to typify the sacred courses of two metaphysical streams (or rivers of energy) entering the symbolic body of the nearby River Wharfe. Such sacred streams became a focus for me in 1982, when I undertook dowsing experiments around the location known as White Wells. Not too far to the east of White Wells, at the back of the Cow & Calf Rocks is the Fairy House. For centuries it was believed by the Ilkley locals to be the domain of the little people, but the best known of all claims to fairy encounters, happened at the old White Wells building in around 1815.

A certain William Butterfield, the respected keeper of the Wells went to open up the healing baths one mid-summer morning. To his amazement, as he tried to enter the large wooden door, he found that his key would not engage in the lock. It simply melted each time her pushed it into the lock, returning to a normal solid key when he took it back out again! Eventually, the door burst open of its own doing and as Butterfield peered into the room of the baths, he couldn't believe what he was looking at. There was a strange humming and buzzing sound which accompanied the other worldly scene opening up in front of his eyes; dozens of small folk, less than a foot in height, dressed all in green from head to foot, were hurrying and scurrying into and out of the waters. Something seemed to indicate Butterfield's presence to them, so they all scampered over the low walls at the rear of the building, off into the vast open moorland.
In December 1987 one of the most celebrated UFO cases took place only meters away from White Wells and this involved very similar entities to those observed by

29

Butterfield over 170 years earlier. The case involved an ex-policeman who claimed that after walking the slopes above White Wells, he turned into a huge crater on the moors. A small green clad entity (which looked like a gnome, but he took to be a space alien) shambled away from him and up into a hovering UFO in the hollow of the crater.

The creature had pointed ears and long spindly arms and was accompanied by an odd humming and buzzing noise, just like the one heard by William Butterfield. The witness, who has never been identified to date, but who was from the Ilkley area, claimed further that he managed to take a photograph of the entity and that in due course, he was actually abducted aboard it's spaceship and taken into the skies above the moors. Is it simply coincidence that both witnesses living over a hundred and fifty years apart, should describe similar (if not the same) kinds of entities observed within a few hundred meters of each other, or is there something else going on here?

At White Wells the ancient spring and well waters originate behind the building which can be seen on the site today and about fifty yards to the east can be found an ancient tumulus that is some fifty feet in diameter. On top of the tumulus are three trees which form a triangle, rising up out of the top of the mound. Along with White Wells, this tumulus is positioned geographically along a line of energy which follows the route of an underground stream. I established that the stream runs north-south by dowsing with a long pendulum, then it continues down into the heart of Ilkley running close to Brooke Street, through the ancient site of the old Parish Church and then to higher ground towards the north of Ilkley, ending in Middleton

Woods, another place said to be haunted by ghosts, fairies and goblins.

Some dowsers claim that they can perceive spirals of earth energies when examining standing stones and at the stone circles on Ilkley Moor. I found this effect quite prominent around the site of the White Wells building. Using a traditional hazel twig as my choice of dowsing instrument, I found that after about twenty visits to the area, I established these same spirals of energy under the ground and marked them out. These energies were nearly always formed in a clockwise orientation, some even passing through the building itself. It seems that this spiraling of the earth's own energy fields, is what is used by something as yet unknown, to manifest the types of entities that have been witnessed in the region and it would seem that the period of time, even hundreds of years, has no factor in this process.

As if to underline that there remains a true mystery at White Wells, it was while I was dowsing there, that I experienced at first had how these manifestations of energy may come about in a quite extraordinary way.

It was March, 1982, I found myself searching out a particular book from the shelves of Ilkley Library that concerned the aforementioned fairy encounter at White Wells. I knew that this little book existed and that it should have been in the library all the time as it was a reference only book. The librarian insisted that the book was still on its particular shelf, but although I looked high and low, I could not find it anywhere. I gave up my search for the book, returning to others that I had been reading on a nearby table. I was somewhat frustrated and annoyed that the book had been taken as its' absence held up my research. Then, I turned sharply to hear a woman's voice, gently saying, *"Is this what you are looking for?"*

The elderly woman reached over my shoulder and took the old brown covered book from the shelves that I had repeatedly searched through only seconds before. I was in utter disbelief, the book was there, directly in front of my own eyes.

Mrs Hill was a kindly old lady, unusual, but in a nice way. On our first meeting over the lost book she had 'found' for me, I began to see her as someone quite special. This was no ordinary person and it soon became evident that she was very psychic. She explained to me that she 'simply knew' where the book was, and that I needed to read it. She invited me to her home which was close to the town in Ilkley, in order to further discuss the topic of the book; the fairies of White Wells.

Upon entering her house, an amazing sight befell my eyes. Paintings depicting all kinds of 'fairy folk', elementals, angels and demons , many , many of them, all spiraling out of the landscape around her picture of White Wells and onto the moors to the south of the baths. This talented artist took little notice as I drew in a gasp at the paintings on the walls of her rooms. It was like a gallery of everything that I had discovered up on those moors. With her, there was just a sense of knowing. She soon told me that the paintings were the result of trance states that she often found herself in most days and I began to wonder if her lovely home made wine may have helped a little, in her reaching such a state of subdued consciousness.

I asked her, "how do you feel in these trances"? She replied that 'she felt very disassociated with reality' and that she could here a strange humming and buzzing sound all around her (again the same sounds that our witnesses to the White Wells phenomenon described in their separate encounter accounts) and that it seemed to take a very short time for her to complete her paintings. She once told me, but never allowed me to test this,

A b/w copy of the original watercolour painting by Mrs Hill (now lost) depicting swirling energies and elementals amidst a woodland scene.

"If you happen to be present when I do my painting, I am sure that I would half ignore you there....but I wouldn't mean to be rude."

It seems the act of 'manifesting ' the paintings into our reality was enough for Mrs Hill to be taken, herself, into another world. Very sadly, Mrs Hill died in 1988, but she left me with a happy reminder of her great talent; a simple water colour called 'Fairies at White Wells'. It depicts elementals, fragile, yet so strong in expression, that they seem to encompass all of the earths energy. They are in flight and the motion draws the eye to the center of the painting, through a great spiral that bursts up from the ground, through the White Wells building, over a nearby tumulus upon which stand three tall trees and, then out...... out, into the tangible world we call reality.

White Wells as seen from the town of Ilkley to the north.

Filling up lost hours that had been previously been taken up in family life, I made my way to the Psychic Fayre being held at the Victoria Hotel in Keighley. Inside, a woman, a complete stranger, came over to me and invited me to accept her offer of a lift home. Finding her attractive, and having been on my own for the past six months, I accepted without hesitation. This woman had an air of knowing about her, strange, yet somehow familiar to me.

The Circle & The Sword

She told me her name, Helju, and very little else about herself, but it became evident that she knew nothing of my personal life -that did not interest her anyway. She spoke little as we drove over the rural network of country roads that connected Keighley with our destination, Chelker Reservoir.

We pulled up in her mini car at the side of the water's edge, a romantic situation, with moonlight reflecting off the surface. Suddenly, as if by some enforced action, Helju turned to me and peered through the darkness of the car's interior, straight into my eyes. She began to speak in a quiet and softly spoken voice, *"Something very ancient is with me Nigel.*

There is a message for you, but we are concerned whether you will be able to accept this at the present time? Are you ready to receive it"?

Helju went very quiet, her breathing becoming hurried, as if she had been overtaken by something outside of her being. This threw me somewhat, and I continued to watch, shaking her arm a little to reassure myself that she was alright. She remained in trance, raised her head, face to face, uttering the words, *"You are to see them in the flesh!..."*

This unexpected statement shook me. I looked away momentarily and back again to see a radiant glow of light that emanated, pouring from her facial features. I could not believe my eyes. Behind her face, like a featureless mask, I made out another, this one without true human form, eye's dark and wide, wise and loving. At the top of its domed head, there seemed to be something positioned from where the light poured out and spiraled into the

35

interior of the car, filling it with a supernatural essence.

*Artists impression of Golden Grey Entity which
appeared to Nigel prior to locating Backstone Circle.*

In April, 1991, during meditation at Backstone Circle, the following words were received. I suspect they originated from the phenomenon, yet seemed to be giving an insight into the make-up of the site and the stones themselves, although of course this has not been proven yet.

The Circle & The Sword

"We have stood as one beneath your skies
A group, yet not as you may find
Cold hearts warmed by that below
Our secrets, Man - a right to know
We watch the land but take no heed
Of human pity fed by greed
Our ancientness, from times to come
A sentinel in the hearts of Man.
Others like us can be found
Now worn and gray by nature's hand
Man's mark upon us, he has borne
To fashion ways of inner- thoughts.
We open doorways in the hope
That all who enter, know as thee
We stand our ground, Our time to come
When all will know that we are One."

CHAPTER TWO

SWORD OF HAKON

Jesus, answering Pilot said, 'My kingdom is not of this world. If my kingdom were of this world, then would my servants fight, that I should not be delivered to the Jews; but now, is my kingdom not from hence? Pilot, therefore said unto him, 'Art thou a king then? Jesus answered, 'thou sayest that I am a king. To this end was I born, and for this cause came I into the world, that I should bear witness unto the truth. Everyone that is of the truth heareth my voice'

'I have not come to bring peace, but a sword' - Mathew 10:34

Less than a quarter of a mile from where Helju and I had sat in her car, the stones of Backstone Circle stood silently, watching over the rolling moorlands. In my mind, I saw the circle site quite clearly, making the connection between its ancientness and the image of the face I had just perceived. The two, although very different, shared something that linked them; a personality that was neither man-made nor natural. There, giving out a vibrant glow, radiant and warm, hanging motionless in mid air, I saw a glorious golden sword! The vision was so real, magnificent in its appearance, that I felt I could have easily reached out and taken a hold of this magical blade. The sword was surrounded by an oval orange disc of light, again equally vibrant and portraying this unusual living quality. The early 1990's saw vision claims of magical and symbolic swords from all over the UK, and 1991 had reports of people visualizing standing stones and dreams of ancient megalithic sites. Was the Earth speaking to us, as some would have it, or was there another answer? The viewpoint taken by Lisa Skinn of Bradford, included that there was a symbolic reverence in the vista; that the sword vision drew attention to the psychological make up of the visioner, in that it revealed through symbolism their personal life quest. This, in view of all that had happened to me so far, I simply could not ignore the possibility that she might be correct? In her response to the sword vision I had experienced, she writes,

"This seems to be the next item on your quest, rising from the Earth Circle, this is an item you must earn and it is never given lightly. You have to show its holder that you have earned the right to bear it. The sword is the symbol of strength, power from within and of course the Truth. This is its mystery -what must be learned, but cannot be taught, that which must be experienced, but cannot be related. It cannot be found in books or on the lips of another. This is your vision, your quest, your truth....and, you alone must learn to live it."

Soon, I had formed for myself a viewpoint concerning my previous OBOL experiences and this vision of the golden sword I had observed at Backstones. After all, I was already on a quest of sorts to find out the truth behind the phenomenon that was already a part of my life, and now it seemed natural to presume that the sword was a part of that quest; something that had been presented to me, a clue, which I had to work out in order to understand any future interactions. No sooner had I chance to reflect upon the sword vision at Backstone Circle, when I came across a written article by no other than Paul Bennett from several years before. He has always been a bit of a local historian, writing for a number of magazines relating to earth mysteries and ancient sites around the north of the UK. In this, he wrote of a legend pertaining to the moorlands surrounding the Bingley region, on the River Aire side of Ilkley Moor.

Included in his notes, was the colourful tale about Athelstan, King of England in 937AD. Visiting Yorkshire en-route to the famous battle at Brunanburh, where he succeeded in defeating King Constantine of Scotland, as well as hordes of Danish marauders. Bennett showed that there were place-name connections with this enigmatic figure, some of them found in the streets and boundary stones still in existence today, like Athestan's Lane in Otley, and The Athel-Stone on Harden Moor, near Keighley. In Athelstan's entourage was his fostre-son

Hakon (also spelling as 'Hakkon'), who had been sent over to England by his father, King Harold Fairhair of Norway. Hakon was not much more than a young teenager when he had to take on his royal responsibilities back in Norway, after his notorious brother Eric Bloodaxe had plundered much of the homeland in greed and power. Despising the cruel rule that his brother and wife Gunnhild of Denmark had forced upon Norway, Hakon swore vengeance, and turned away from the darker pagan witchcraft that evil-hearted Eric and Gunnhild were practicing.

Photograph of Garry Hubert standing next to the memorial stone for his ancestor King Hakon The Good, near the burial mound at Seim, Bergen Norway.

On his return to Norway as King of all the land, Hakon was muchloved by his peoples who came to call him Hakon The Good. It seems that they had Athelstan to thank for that, who had taken a liking to young Hakon, teaching him the ways of a king who although still pagan in some respects, yet blithe of temper, well spoken in the

English dialect, and wiser than most, instilled the Christian doctrines in him. Athelestan's court, at either Wessex or in York, was the place where Hakon was christened by Athelstan; so loved by his foster father was the youth, that he gave him a magnificent sword for his personal use.

This sword is interesting. It may have been one of the many sacred relics said to have been collected by Athelstan from all over Europe. It is written in the Norse saga's that, *'it was the grandest of all swords to enter Norway, and was so powerful, that it could cut straight through hard stone with one clean stroke!'* Here we have tentative connections with King Arthur's magical Excalibur -the sword given to the boy-king by Merlin. Hakon's sword had a name too, so famous was it in his time, called Quernbiter (pronounced Kwern-bitter). Legend had it that wielding the weapon, Hakon could cleave a quern, a kind of circular stone corn grinder, with a single stroke and with so much accuracy that he hit the center eye of the quern every time. There must have been something remarkable about this young prince, even in his youth, that King Athelstan saw in him. He rode at the right hand side of the King, and was special enough, as to have been given the enigmatic Quernbitter, with all its supposed magical properties. I feel this had to do with Hakon himself, the person, someone who wielded and used humanistic qualities and understanding that was way ahead of his time.

Yes, Hakon was a real person. He exists in history and his

life is known about, unlike the legendary figure of King
Arthur, with his sword Excalibur, he has descendants who
are alive today, proud of the heritage bestowed upon them
by this famous king of Norway. It is without a shadow of
doubt, that Hakon learned enough during his time with
Athelstan in England, to be able to become a renowned
figure in his home country after the death of his father
King Harold Fairhair. Whilst in England, at a young age,
Hakon was taught the principles of early Christianity,
something of a mystery in itself, for this Pagan ruler from
overseas. His life was a constant battle between this new
found worship of the one God, with his own beliefs
surrounding the Norse Gods. Even when he finally
returned to his homeland, to overthrow his evil brother,
Eric the Red -who had ideas on gaining the throne for
himself - Hakon tried in vain to establish Christianity
amongst his own people, only to fail himself in this
endeavor, and returning to Pagan worship shortly before
his death. Even so, Hakon kept parts of the new religion
alive in his political laws in Norway. He was wise and knew
that he had to compromise, knowing that it would be a
long journey and struggle to convert all pagans to this new
religion, and this would not happen overnight.

There was a sense of good and righteousness about
Hakon, and his people saw that he was a just man. The
Eddas write of him as a hero, not just in battle, but in
everyday life too. Even today, some of the most important

political laws of Norway, were founded by *'Hakon the Good'*. It would be a fancy of thought to think that there really was such a blade in existence at that time, which had the extra-ordinary power to be able to accomplish this impossible feat attributed to Quernbiter, so we should look at this legendary tale, as possibly a allegorical representation of something else. As we have already discussed, swords were often thought to have held their own qualities of strength and personality. Swords were depicted as being holders of the truth, strength, righteousness, and good; all qualities that the owner would have liked to have been reflective of themselves. We see this clearly with Hakon's sword cutting straight through to the center-eye. In this kind of thinking, we could say that the center-eye symbolised the 'psychic eye', the center of inner knowledge, the all-knowing eye.

The year was 932AD, England ravished by the inner turmoil of war after war brought to its shores by the Danish Viking invaders. Unity had to be sought in a land divided, if there was ever to be a return to the splendor of the 'magical Isles of Albion'. The Dark Ages had severely split the country, its' leaders succumbing to joint rule between the Danelaw and survivors of the Anglo-Saxon reign. Athelstan set out from Wessex in the south to attack the King of the Picts on Scotland's boarders, in an attempt to reunite England under one leadership under the banner of the Christian God. Along the journey north, he crossed the River Humber and called at Beverley Minster, before passing on to the city of York. It was whilst at Beverley, that he knelt at the tomb of St. John laying a short-sword at the alter, promising to God that he would redeem it after the battle. (He also left swords at York, and copies of the gospels at the church of Chester-Le-Street.)

Continuing his march, Athelstan defeated the Picts, and on the return, he made the location of the minster a free-hold to those that had done wrong; a kind of place of mercy or sanctuary. To mark the boundary for this safe-haven, he instructed there to be erected four marker stones on the outskirts of the township at a mile distance between. Even today, it is sometimes presumed that churches offer a place of safe-keeping for those on the run from injustice, and this reflects Athelstan's law.

Eventually, Athelstan centered his rule of the country in York. Today on a clear day, it is possible to see the towers of the minster of York from the top of Ilkley Moor. Unfortunately, there is no firm historical record to show whether Athelstan ever visited Ilkley Moor, but it does seem likely that he would have been familiar with the Wharfedale region. Before his time, there had been important Roman garrisons at Otley and Ilkley, then later, Anglo-Saxon and Viking communities spread throughout the Yorkshire dales. At Ilkley Church there are three beautifully carved stone crosses (that can be found inside the building now) which date to 770-870 AD. The high quality of these carvings suggest that the site may have been a pre-viking monastery. We cannot ignore the connection the Bingley area had with Hakon and the legend of the sword, Quernbiter. The thoughts of some kind of Thor-like Viking warrior on his mount, wielding the mother of all swords and slicing standing stones like they were made out of butter, seems far too fantastic anywhere, least of all on Ilkley Moor! But, the story had to originate somewhere. Like all legends, there is usually some truth at the core of it all. Maybe we need to look at this 'center-eye' aspect of the legend again, for that has been a title often given to the region for which Ilkley Moor is a part of.

Rombalds Moor, named after the legendary Giant Rombald (himself, a corruption of earlier accounts in which Satan was said to have been roaming the night skies over these Yorkshire moorlands; itself, an attempt to explain away the strange lights that were being observed there) can be found to be geographically central to England. Here, in 'God's own country', is it any coincidence that there can be found more examples of megalithic stone carvings, cup and ring stones, stone circles, and standing stones, in six square miles of open moorland than anywhere else in the UK? In early times, there was something very important about Rombalds Moor, and early man knew this. Was this England's 'center-eye' - the physical and spiritual soul of the country? If this place was a focus for such, then maybe an early center for religion too, and then there should be some kind of evidence for it. Well, I have shown how the OBOL phenomenon and visionary experiences brought me to the realisation that there is something unique about the moor, and we only have to reach back to the 1930s to see that this 'strange attraction of the moor' had been noticed before.

The Lands of the Dragon

There is an area to the north of Ilkley town which in past years was secretively regarded by occultists as 'the lands of the dragon'. You will not find this location in any published manuscript, yet from one source, an unpublished script (in part, the lost and forgotten spell book of Lord Henry Clifford of Skipton, that was remarkably discovered in a waste skip in Baildon by a certain Daniel Murgatroyd) this place is described in mysterious and enigmatic fashion. Indeed, included within this secret script is an actual map depicting the boundaries of this supposed magical landscape.

Before I ever saw this information, I had been for some time through my own UFO and paranormal investigations, reaching a conclusion that there was something very special about that very place. I had visited it many times, unaware that throughout history, it had been regarded by visionaries, alchemists, Freemasons and the like, as some kind of supernatural mecca. This open lonely moorland, bordering the township and hamlets of Bingley known as the lands of the dragon, is the location, where in ages past, Prince Hakon's sword made its legendary appearance.

Although the name of this area sounds like something right out of the pages of Tolkien, the Lands of the Dragon are a very real place. Situated some 12 miles south of the city of Bradford, West Yorkshire, it is an area of no more than six to seven square miles, predominantly made up of open moorland and rugged terrain. With giant rock outcrops, meandering ancient trackways, and Neolithic settlements, it still holds an air of mystery, desolation and other worldly qualities. The place has never changed since early man roamed there, and evidence of his megalithic heritage can still be found in the way of stone-circles, standing stones and druid temples. We are of course, dealing with Ilkley Moor.Daniel Murgatroyd's secret document of Sir Henry Cliffords spell book, contained a map, drawn by hand, of the supposed placement of the Lands of the Dragon. From it, we can see that the area in question is surrounded by three towns found in Airedale and Wharfedale: Skipton, Keighley, and Bingley. To the direct north of these, we find Bolton Abbey (near Ilkley), the Swastika Stone found on Ilkley Moor, and the village of Baildon. On the original document, symbols were used to depict each of these places: Skipton -a castle, Keighley - a lamp as found on the cross there in the market place, Bingley- an open book, Baildon - the fire of Baal (Baildon derives its name from Baal -don), the swastika at Ilkley, and an Abbey at Bolton. All of these places can still be found on maps today, they circle the moorland that lays between them. All hold tentative clues as to the lost mystery of the Lands of the Dragon, and the question has arisen, why should such a barren moorland be important enough as to have been emphasised in Murgatroyd's cryptic manuscript? Without a shadow of doubt, this area is the high plateau between the rivers Aire & Wharfe, which is called Rombald's Moor.

A bound copy of Daniel Murgatroyd's book, 'The Lands o the Dragon' showing spiral, swasika stone, and the dragon.

I wondered why this place should have been called the Lands of the Dragon. Could it simply have been a reference to a long lost legend of a dragon tale from those moors, like others found around the Yorkshire region. A little research shows, however, there are numerous links with dragon symbolism in this area. Both crests of the townships of Skipton and Keighley have within their design dragons. The Keighley crest has a dragon's head with a coiled serpent around it, whilst the crest of Skipton shows a dragon holding a flag, upon which can be found an image of Skipton Castle built by the Clifford family. Henry Clifford - alchemist, was a member of this family and we shall explore his strange links with nearby Bolton Abbey in due course.

Between Skipton and Keighley is a place called Cliffe Castle. Here, again we find dragon symbolism linking the Clifford family with the building and its site. Dragon heads can be seen carved atop the pillars of the great doorway into Cliffe Castle. Even today, dragon symbols seem to abound in Keighley. There is the colorful mosaic to be found tiled into the footpath at Cross Green, not far from the Cross as depicted in Murgatroyd's map. Even the railway station is ornamented with carvings of dragons.

Henry Clifford's Dragon Lore

Lord Henry Clifford was a strange & odd person. A star gazer and alchemist of medieval times, he was also the

Lord of Skipton Castle. It is said that he used to meet with his coven at a secret meeting place on the high reaches of Ilkley moor, which along a major energy path linked the earth to the sky. Today, we know this place to be the ancient site of the Twelve Apostles stone circle. During his early life Henry Clifford spent a part of his time as a recluse, locking himself away in Barden Tower, less than a mile from Bolton Abbey. Apart from his wanderings around the Yorkshire countryside between Bolton and Ilkley Moor, where he got the reputation of being called *'the Shepherd Lord'* (due to alleged reports that he was able to communicate with animals in the wild), Henry was known to have mapped stars and celestial bodies, often positioned over the open moorlands to the south. Through alchemy and delving into the lost arts of the Black Cannons of Bolton Priory, who taught him their 'secret wisdom and knowledge', forbidden by the church, it seems that Henry was searching for something more physically lost and hidden in the Ilkley Moor region. It may have been around this time, 1510 AD, that the mysterious Lord of Skipton Castle began to write up his secret spell book; the one eventually discovered by Daniel Murgatroyd over four centuries later in a rubbish pile.

Whatever hidden knowledge Lord Henry Clifford obtained during his time at Barden Tower, evidence remains today that when the foundation stones were being built for the priory at nearby Bolton, it was deemed necessary that carvings of a strange swastika motif should be included upon them. In fact, there are literally dozens of these swastika symbols, smaller in size, but exactly the same in design as the one found on the craggy slopes of Ilkley Moor, carved all around the base of Bolton Abbey. Someone, at the time of the building's construction, wanted it to be recognised that the priory had links with this particular ancient site on the moors. What those links were remained a hidden mystery.

> 'Among the shepherd-grooms, no mate
> Had he—a child of strength and state,
> Among the heavens his eye could see
> Face of thing that is to be;
> And, if man report him right,
> He could whisper words of might.'
> **Wordsworth**

The Circle & The Sword

Lunds Tower, near Sutton, West Yorkshire.

Skipton's crest (coat of arms), along with the red dragon motif, was derived from the heraldic coat of arms associated with the Clifford family. Only a few miles from Skipton, on the outskirts of Keighley is the enigmatic building called Cliffe Castle. Built upon the preexisting site of Cliffe Hall, this building isn't a castle at all in the true sense of the word. It is one of the last Victorian' follies, remaining today as a council run museum and tourist attraction. Cliffe Castle has undergone a series of re-developments and structural extensions down the past years. Recent work on the entrance walls, has uncovered lost painted images, which had been covered up previously. These depict a dragon-like creature, said to represent the Griffin.

These mythical creatures found gold in the mountains and built their nests of it, for which reason their nests were very tempting to the hunters, and they were forced to keep vigilant guard over them. Their instinct led them to know where buried treasures lay, and they did their best to keep plunderers at a distance. Can we dare to imagine that the original owners of Cliffe Castle should choose this symbolic dragon-like creature to represent their own 'quest' to find some long lost and buried treasure in the locality, and at the same time indebted to keep this a covert secret. Could the location of such a treasure be close by, maybe within view of the castle? Looking due north-west of Cliffe Castle, in clear view is the open expanse of Ilkley Moor; at the heart of the 'Lands of the Dragon'. This seems much more than coincidence.

Only a few miles east of Skipton, can be found the village of Glusburn. Hanging over this village, upon a craggy outcrop, is the looming Lunds Tower. Local legend states that a sleeping dragon lies in wait underneath the tower, and this reminds one of the famous British legend of Llud. In pre-Roman times, Britain was afflicted by three plagues. One was an invasion by a sinister folk with magic powers, the second a terrible noise that drove people mad, and the third a famine. Llud, the son of Heli, was said to be a fanatical planner and builder and in his attempt to overcome the plagues in his land, he used cunning and wisdom. In the case of the second plague, the terrible shriek, this was caused by the roar of a 'British dragon' as it fought with a foreign one at the exact center of the Country. Llud had to locate them both (some accounts say in the Oxford area). He found the dragons in a pit in the center of the country, and lowered a vessel of mead with a silken cover over it. The dragons in their fighting, fell onto the mead and drank of it, falling into a stupor. Llud covered the dragons with the silk cover and entombed them in a stone coffin, buried under the ground somewhere in Snowdonia.

The legend continues, that Vortigen, trying to build a stronghold against the invading Saxons, noticed that his building kept falling down for no apparent reason. Wise men told him that he should make a sacrifice of a boy to virgin birth. Such a boy was eventually found, a seer, who told Vortigen that the subsidence was due to an underground pool in which two great dragons, a red and a white one, lay in it. These were the monsters put there by Llud years before. Interestingly, the region described as the Lands of the Dragon lay geographically at the center of England. We can now establish that the 'Lands of the Dragon' is certainly the Rombalds Moor area, Ilkley Moor as part of Rombalds Moor, being a major section of this landscape.

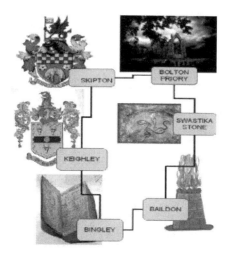

Diagram by the author showing the towns surrounding the lands of the drgon with the Swastika Stone on Rombalds Moor at the center.

A local businessman, Nicholas Size found 'the lands of the dragon' such a powerful place, that he wrote of his own experiences in a book he titled, 'The Haunted Moor' (1934). From his accounts he writes,

'The feeling that I had been there (Ilkley Moor) before always intrigued me, and about this time I read some of the literature of the Theosophical Society, and learned that many other people had at different times shared my experience, in one place or another, of feeling that they

had seen the place before, when in point of fact they were seeing it for the first time. The theosophists explain that this phenomenon is due to our having veritably seen the place before in some previous incarnation, and it is fair to say that some similar view is held by multitudes of people in India and elsewhere. Also the theosophists suggest that at times our own spirits visit new places in our dreams and half remember them, so that when we encounter them for the first time we have really (in a way) seen them before.'

What I found amazing when I first came across Size's book in the Ilkley Public Library in 1982, was how his accounts mirrored many modern day experiences that have been reported from those enigmatic moors. Even the locations that Size writes about, are the very same ones where similar encounters have occurred in more recent years - underlining my speculations that the origin of the phenomena that is being witnessed there, lays somewhere between the human psyche and the geophysical make up of the moor itself. It seems that Size always sensed himself to be a part of the moor and found its' calling at times, irresistible. He colors for the reader his treks out of the Ilkley township up onto the reaches behind White Wells. An area he began to regard as the Place of Horrors.

It is still possible to retrace his footsteps along the rocky crag ways and seek out for oneself the places where Size claimed his interactions with the unknown. Size was interested in the many marked rocks as well as the cup and ring stones on the moor. It was believed that Neolithic Man roamed the moorlands in this area, building their stone monuments to whichever gods they worshiped at that time; most probably a solar deity. On one occasion, Size walked by the huge rock beyond the Cow and Calf Rock (most likely to be West Rock which was known to be a site of ancient sacrificial rituals) when, quite unexpectedly, ghostly figures came forth out of the ground mist. Each of these, held a flame-like torch above its head and Size noticed an odd phosphorescence surrounding the rocks nearby. Size remarked,

'to all intents and purposes, the whole scene looked like something that had been opened up to reveal the distant past'.

"You are not real", screamed Size! As he watches, he feels that his whole being has no purpose and he is losing control of his whereabouts. In this confused state he goes on, "my hands and feet seemed fastened in some way and I was hauled and lifted by invisible hands that were irresistible...." As he battled with his wits, Size got the impression that something had been implanted in his head by the power that was now leading him on. He looked around in a haze across the valley below and across to Armscliffe Cragg on the north-eastern horizon, the vision-like experience beginning to fade, but his forgotten memories of the previous night he had spent on those moors came flooding back to him; a luminous cloud had

58

been hanging over the Cragg, *'very much like the Pleiades, but singularly low in the sky'*.

The more he thought about this, Size realised that the lights above the Cragg and those he had seen with the ghostly images on Ilkley Moor, were somehow signaling to one another like *'some strange rites that were common to both'*.

Size was about 40 years old at the time he wrote about Ilkley Moor, after traveling the world; all in all, a quite learned man, not easily fooled it seems by simple tricks of the light that might spook the unaware rambler. That said, he outlines with feeling, how certain areas of the moor made him feel uneasy, like the region where there remains today a stretch of trees on the northern slopes behind the old wells building. Is it nothing more than coincidence that even today reports of strange lights and unusual time-anomalies frequent the very same spot on the moor. Equally, there are areas of the moor, which give the complete opposite feeling to that found by Size and others down the years. Clues can be found in some of the location names, such as White Wells - denoting a place with positive connotations, i.e. the colour white, good, a place of healing qualities, etc. In fact, it seems that the energies' found on the moor, call it the atmosphere of the place, is constantly changing between positive and negative influences. Even White Wells was known to have been a *'cold and sullen place'* at the turn of the last century, when the location then became the haunt of thieves, murderers and other wrong-doers. This is interesting because it shows that reputations about these places, are not static, but arise from the perceptions of those who come into contact with these sites at different times in history.

There may have been a reputation that Ilkley Moor was the geographical & magical center-eye of England during the Dark Ages. And, there is another reason why we should regard the area as being 'special', so to speak. That can be found in the enigmatic rock carving known as the Swastika Stone. Unlike many of the cup and ring carved rocks to be found on the central moor, the Swastika Stone is unique. Nobody has ever worked out just what its true meaning is, or was. Archaeologists date the design to the Bronze Age at least, but it may in fact, derive from a much earlier period in history. It seems to be a corruption of the cross – symbol with added details, incorporating the arms of the Solar Wheel of the Sun God, Baal. The swastika form is universal and there are other designs of this kind found all over the world, but the one at Woodhouse Crag, Ilkley, has a strange hooked tail ending in a single cup shaped hollow. This swastika is in effect, a representation of the 'god force' or Creation forces that are responsible for our sense of reality. So, what is it doing here, positioned on the edge of moorland, overlooking the Ilkley township in the vale below. What did the originators of the carving know, and what were they trying to tell us?

Photograph shows the relica of the Swastika Stone carved on a rock next to the original which is so erroded with age.

In the 1950's, a world-famous UFO Contactee, George Adamski claimed that Venusian pilots had given him evidence of their reality, in the shape of photographic plates, on which were depictions of strange shapes and hieroglyphics. Adamski's contact with these angelic beings took place in the Californian deserts of the USA, and although he did tour the world to promote his book, *Flying Saucers Have Landed*, he never visited anywhere in England. Very strange then, that we find the exact swastika design on the plates that were given to Adamski, as that found on Ilkley's Swastika Stone. Even the odd looking tail design is there for all to see. Coincidence?

Time Lapse at the Swastika Stone

This is quite the most remarkable UFO case to come from

this area of Ilkley Moor. Some twenty four years after the event, all three witnesses to what happened talk about it as if it happened yesterday. George Annings was one of the three middle aged visitors who attended an outing organised by a spiritualist church in Leeds. The other two, were both women in their late forties and they had all become friends through their shared interest in spiritualism. George relates what happened to them in 1983.

'Our visit to the Swastika Stone was made in the early Autumn of that year and on that occasion I arrived at the church in Leeds, only to discover that our leader had been notified of several absences due to illness. There was going to be only the three of us at the meeting, so on the spur of the moment, we decided to take a trip to Ilkley Moor. We left Leeds at around 7.00pm and drove straight to the moors which took a further half hour. After parking the car, we set off on foot to look for the ancient site of the stone and followed a track over two small streams that were easy to stride over at Hebers Ghyll. Eventually we reached the outcrop of rocks where the carving is found. It was still quite light in the evening around 7.45pm, when we all sat down at the side of the Swastika Stone and began to close our eyes in meditation.

Sketch of the swastika stone by the author in 1990.

'I then fell asleep and as far as I know, so did my other
two friends. After what seemed an instant, we all awoke
together and none of us could work out what had
happened. We were puzzled and confused, we did not
know how long we had been asleep, but it was now getting
very dark. The darkness of night was everywhere which
made our situation even more frightening for us. There
was an eerie silence all around. We found it difficult to
make out where we stood and this worried me more
because I knew we were positioned close to a fifty foot
sheer drop off the edge of the moors.

'My two friends began to panic and held on to one

another, I had nothing to offer them in the way of comfort because I did not know what had just taken place. It was utter confusion. Then, some moments later, we could all see a bright ball of bright white light that just hung in the air close to our position. It was the only source of light that we could see, but it did not illuminate much of the ground around us at first. I took this to be a rescuing helicopter that had spotted us lost on the moor, but then I had to reconsider this option, as there was no sound coming from the object and it was by now quite close to us. I could see that the light was not like a beam, but a bubble of daylight in the vast blackness of the open moorland sky. Due to its close proximity, all three of us ruled out the possibility that it was the Moon -this was more oval and full of light, looking to be at its closest, at rooftop height. I know this sounds peculiar, but we all felt a calming feeling when we looked at it, which seemed to convince us that it was not going to harm any of us.

'We felt safe with it, even though we did not know what it was? So, we decided to walk, nervously, towards the ball of light in a direction that would take us away from the track back to the parked up car. We began to move ahead, all the time the ball of light in the form of this 'bubble' kept moving slightly forwards and we were then able to see a little further along our route across the dangerous moorland terrain. I would still have to see a map of the location, to see what path we were led to take, but in time it became clear to us that the ball of light was playing a *game of 'follow my leader' (crossing two streams, clambering over wet glassy rocks in a disorientated state due to the bright light from the UFO reflecting off the water in the darkness) and in doing so, we were led eventually back to our car.*

'Having reached the safety of the car, the women in tears, I looked up to see what was happening with the ball of light? It was gone in a flash, but left us with another puzzle in that over three hours had elapsed since we fell asleep at the Swastika Stone. This was impossible! It was now well after 11.00pm and no matter how we tried to account for this missing time on our hurried journey home to Leeds, there was no way that what we had experienced would have taken that amount of time.'

Although these two cases seem to be extreme examples of how the OBOL phenomenon operates, there are many more cases from all over the world which demonstrate there is a personal connection of awareness between the sighting and the witness to it. In her book 'Alien Contact', ufologist, Jenny Randles describes how Gaynor Sunderland and other members of her family, *'after initial UFO encounters in Wales',* began to delve deeply into psychic matters. In the months preceding May, 1980, Gaynor had already claimed that she had observed UFOs and even alien entities at close range several times. However, on the night of the 28th May, her mother, Marion, set off out of their house in Oakenhalt for her usual late night walk. Looking over towards the skies above a nearby mountain, she watched as a huge ball of orange light hung silently in the darkness of the sky. At midnight, after returning indoors, she noticed that the UFO was still there, *'maintaining its silent vigil like a guardian angel'*.

How apt, these words written by Jenny in her book. Were the two OBOLs seen and then photographed at the villages of Addingham and Appletreewick, indeed, representations of *'guardian angels'*? After her alien contacts, it seems that a latent psychic ability within Gaynor suddenly magnified, just as it had done so in my own case. She began to explore ways to communicate with this, and as it seems her mother Marion already had an interest in ancient sites and standing stones, Gaynor in due course, started delving into historical questing with the help of her friend, Andrew Collins. Questing - the undertaking of seeking out lost or hidden objects and information through psychic means - was certainly put on the paranormal map through the teaming up of the Sunderlands and Collins during the early 1980s. Andrew had initially started working with Gaynor as a UFO/Paranormal investigator, but his own passion for deeper occult ways to identify any meaning in her experiences, soon led to a growing interest around the UK in psychic questing. Obviously these cases are just a few examples of how these enigmatic OBOL encounters seem to have a direct effect upon the lives and later attitudes of those who experience such, and there are many more which would easily fill this works alone. It is clear that we are not simply dealing with nuts and bolts spacecraft here; the repeated psychic element pointing to something which would suggest much more happening that is difficult to fully understand.

The OBOL experience, however, is a precedent to the arousal of deeper psychic awareness in witnesses, many of whom do go on to develop their own psychic abilities, usually due to an almost obsessive seeking to better understand the initial encounters, but also to interact on this level further and in doing so, trying to re-establish a contact with the source of the phenomenon. Intuitively, there is a knowing involved here. This, at the start, is very hard to grasp by these 'questors of the truth', and many avenues of thought, suppositions, and false leads, can make this a difficult time to progress psychically through. Yet, they feel within, this hidden knowing. It is as if the answer to their own involvement in something quite incredible, lay hidden in a part of themselves which everyday life finds very hard to reach, let alone understand.

The early 1990's were for me a strange mix of emotional extremes. I had married for a second time, but like the first this was doomed to end with much heartbreak for all concerned. After lessons learned from my first marriage, I made it very clear from the start, what Debs, my wife then, would be letting herself in for, but the stigma of 'believing' in things that for most are completely out of their reach of understanding, was probably the main ingredient in our loving demise. Being very sensitive (this seems to be a cursing attribute of the truthseeker) and living each day as if on a mission, takes one away from the normality of our accustomed social life expectations. I seemed to be very over-sensitive to little things with Debs at times, and lo and behold her, if she should lie at all, even a small lie.....That was something I simply could not bare. All that ever mattered was 'truth'... I even found this odd myself, as I had always been a quiet, fair and none-judgmental person. That was pre-1980 of course.

No, there seemed to be something else, that was driving me on, something that I had little choice in, something that was coloring my life in the way that it wanted it to be like for me, and I found questioning this an impossible act. The relationship with Debs brought me two great boys, and although there were extremely bad times, equally the good ones brought about a strange sort of balance. Yet, within, we both knew that we were living out a false marriage. Our days were numbered and something within me would not allow this to change. I was very down a lot of the time. In fact, I would say that I was suffering depression, and I began to look elsewhere for the solace and love that was rapidly exiting my life. Loneliness overcame me day after day. Debs and I had stopped talking to each other, making home-life impossible, and all I wanted to do was rekindle the love we had known, but with time, I knew inwardly that I was being taken away from her and there would be no way that this could be turned around again. Stumbling through the autumn days of 1990, I found myself alone at Ilkley Parish Church seeking answers.

Earlier in the day, I had been out with newspaper reporters for the Bradford Telegraph & Argus, shooting photo's to be used in conjunction with a piece they were running on local UFO encounters. I half-heatedly assisted them with this, but really didn't feel I had anything to offer them at the time. Later, around mid day, I ventured back down into Ilkley and roamed, alone and with only my own thoughts to comfort me, around empty streets. The weather was the worst I had known it; a never ceasing drizzle of rain, almost mist-like, covered everything. It was cold and dull and heavy black clouds filled the overcast skies above. Certainly not the picture postcard scene so often painted of Ilkley. Although I had lived in the Ilkley area for the best part of a decade, it did not surprise me to find those streets empty. No one I knew would be around to chat to -you know, it's a kind of feeling you get, when fate dictates that you will be alone, no matter what? So, I wandered on, trudging the streets, peering into shop windows with a blinded half hearted gaze, crossed over to the church, and wondered why? Looking up at the cold stone church did nothing to quell the feelings of emptiness within me, there was no sense of being at one with my God here, no friends, and a complete dislike of what I had become. I realised in those moments, that I had lost the real me, that had been taken away back in 1980, and all that was left now, was an empty shell, a body that carried someone that I did not know, and more to the point, someone I did not want to be. I should think that it is when you reach these low points in life, that you get the chance to examine yourself; where you have been, what you have done, and maybe, where you are going? All I did, without reflection and unashamed selfishness, was to continue to demand why?

I lifted the 35mm camera to eye level and peered through the viewfinder, scanning the outer walling of the church for something that might interest me. Emotion welled up inside me and in a moment I knew that I was at my lowest ever in the whole of my life. Why do we struggle on, is it all worth it in the end? I had no answers for such open-ended questions of the heart. *"If there is any point to all of this, show me now..."*, the words tripped off a tongue under bated breath. I jerked the camera upwards with a seemingly involuntary action, and equally so, I pressed down the shutter, not knowing what I had captured on the film, if anything at all?

This church has had links with the reported UFO sightings around Ilkley, mainly involving the OBOL kinds of phenomena. In March, 1982, a hospital mini-bus from nearby Middleton stopped at the traffic lights at the top of Brook Street, adjacent and to the left of the church. It was about 8.00pm in the evening. A nurse traveling on the bus, noticed a lighted area above the clock tower, which she saw as an orange 'sun-like' ball of light about 20 feet above the rooftop. She watched with a friend, as the tennis-ball sized OBOL moved away at a slow pace, but each time they started to walk, it stood stationary in the sky. It mimicked their movements three times, before vanishing from sight.

Two years later, on 8th July, 1984, we had the great fire at York Minster, and again there were reports of strange OBOL phenomena being associated with the disaster. Believers in the faith, claimed that the fire had been an act of God, his punishment for the blasphemous statements given by retired Rev. David Jenkins, who stated that both the virgin birth of Christ and the resurrection were falsehoods. Yet, on the eve of the fire, several witnesses came forward to say that they had observed a huge ball of orange light, which shot out a flame that hit the roof of the minster. Adding to this confusion, there was a report of a gray cigar-shaped UFO in the vicinity at the time of the fire.

By now, I was becoming something of a celebrity in the UFO groups world, I had been lecturing on the subject around the UK, and gave several TV appearances. I met with famous names like Uri Geller and Toyah Wilcox. I worked hard to bring out the truth about the experiences that people were having, normal people like myself, people with lives, with problems and with dreams. I was on the scales of my life, on the one hand, I was sinking ever deeper in my love life into an abyss, and on the other, I was elevated to the heights of egotistical fame of sorts. But, no matter how hard I tried, there was no balance here. It seemed that I could not be happy in both landscapes. The straw that broke the camels back and then the end of my marriage to Debs, came in a way that brought all the absurdity of how dramatically my life had changed fully into focus.

Headlines in the Ilkley Gazette read,

'Three Year UFO Mystery Exposed as a Hoax'

A three-year UFO mystery involving a lump of rock and a bottle of alcoholic lemonade has finally been exposed as a hoax. X-files boffin Nigel Mortimer, who regularly leads enthusiasts on UFO spotting missions on Ilkley Moor, received bizarre maps telling him where to find supposed alien relics which would become the Eighth Wonder of the World. He said: *"As a ufologist I am constantly open to hoaxes and pranks but this has gone on for far too long."* The hoax began three years ago when Nigel received an anonymous map with weird markings on it, relating to UFO mysteries. Last August events took on a more sinister tone when a second map making references to a mysterious alien relic, The Mog Stone, arrived through Nigel's letterbox. Although he suspected the map may have been a hoax, Nigel made it a priority to find out if the truth really was out there. He said: *"I think anyone who believes their home is being watched by someone unknown, or from outer space, would be concerned."* Further documents and letters about The Mog Stone arrived at Nigel's home, one even claiming the stone would be the Eighth Wonder of the World. Unconvinced, Nigel enlisted fellow ufologist Jon Hurst, for help in tracing the source. He set up a new UFO internet site as a trap and almost immediately a message regarding the Mog Stone appeared. The message was traced back to the business address of Frazer Irwin, an outspoken resident of Ilkley. When confronted he admitted to the hoax. He said, *"The Mog Stone is a fake. It's actually a lump of rock, named after alcoholic lemonade, which I have been hiding in my wardrobe. I made it look like a head and intended to reveal it as an April Fool"* Nigel said Mr Irwin had overstepped the mark. Unwittingly, Fraser Irwin had no idea how this had effected my life at home. Things were already fragile to say the least, but the day to day worries of someone keeping a watch over you, was for Debs too much. I could see her worry, and because of how things were, there was little I could say to her to re-assure her. She began to see every car that parked up outside the house as a threat because there were references on the maps to parts of my life, and places where I had previously lived, even before I encountered the OBOL in 1980; to which I have never received a satisfactory explanation from Irwin.

Nigel Mortimer

Leaving home for a second time, was hard for me.
Leaving behind my two young boys (not in a physical
sense as I have always kept contact with them, but through
the 'knowing' of not being with them at home everyday) ,
even harder, but there was no choice in the matter for me.
I searched within myself, endlessly, for the reasons I had
to be involved in this 'thing' -a curse of kinds, that led me
onwards to some place where I couldn't take others. I was
on my lone quest again, so I searched deeper than I have
ever done before, and within the depths of solitude, I
found something that until then, I had overlooked. It
began one month before I moved into my new home in
Menston, I suddenly became aware of a presence within,
that was prepared to listen. It was not a part of myself, but
came and went at will. Was I losing my marbles? Was I
going mad? I questioned this over and over again, then
the answer arrived on my very doorstep. I opened the
packet which the postman had placed through the
letterbox, and flicked through the enclosed set   of
photographs. Most were of local scenes, some of the
family, and two or three of around Ilkley. One of these,
was the photograph I had taken involuntarily at the Ilkley
parish church. I looked once at it, then again and nearly
dropped it onto the floor! My mouth dropped open to
match it. There, in front of my own eyes, I saw clearly an
image made from the cloud formations in the print.
Hanging right above the clock tower of the church,
looking down with serious intent, was the unmistakable

face of a Viking warrior, bearded and wearing a typical helmet of the period. There was a sense of familiarity about this person, and as I inspected the photograph more closely, I knew within myself, that although it seemed impossible, I was looking into the very face of Hakon himself. A few days later, I met up with Paul Bennett to let him have a look at the photograph. During our conversations, he began to tell me about myths and legends from the area above Otley, where I had first encountered the OBOL in 1980, in particular the story of the Timble Witches. The witches were really locals of the Norwood Valley, who, having survived the ravishes of the Civil War, became relations to the wealthy landowners known to Edward Fairfax.

Fairfax became a kind of witch finder general in the region, after finding that his own daughter had become the target of the witches -or so she claimed. In truth, it seems that these witches were holding firm the remembrances of the old pre-Christian traditions, some of which had been at the core of this small and closely knit community, tucked away from the more modern lives of the progressive townships. Anyway according to the story, one evening the Timble witches gathered in one of the houses for a very important reason, never yet disclosed, or kept hidden and lost to time. When gathered together, they all set off out over the track-ways and open fields, through village hamlets and climbing the rocky cliffs and raging streams, until they arrived at their goal, Ilkley Moor! At the same time, this was taking place, on the other side of the Pennines, in Lancashire, other witches gathered and headed out to the same moor. Meeting at the 'highest part of the moor' (possibly somewhere near to the Twelve Apostles stone circle), it seems that their intent was to seek out a source of immense power, which they sought to gain for themselves

A b/w copy of the photograph taken by the author of Ilkley Church, showing the face of 'Haakon' looking down onto it!

I began to research what Paul had told me concerning these night flights to Ilkley Moor by these witches, and although any evidence was sparse, I did find tentative clues in Fairfaxs' works: this excursion of Helen Fairfax and the witches was in an easterly direction from Newhall (at Otley), down the valley of the Washburn towards Rowton

Bridge, there across the water, up the other side of the valley into Norwood, then passing near Bland Hill, then across Braime Lane leading on the high road, then out upon the open moor." (*Deamonologia- Grainge 1882*)

During the journey, their route took them close to one of the highest landmarks within the Washburn locality called Bland Hill, and within yards of this, we find a raised area, almost pointed in its nature, named of all things.... *'Sword Point'.*

A cup & ring marked stone is positioned such on Ilkley Moor that it points towards the crater where an aledged alien abduction took place in 1987. It lays along the line from Sword Point.

Paul and I stared at each other in disbelief, grabbed the OS map, and traced the line of route again. We found that not only did Sword Point suggest a solid connection with an ancient relic or weapon, its situation suggested by the lay of the land, that the continuous peaking ending in a point overlooking the region, and this was pointing in the same direction as that taken by the Timble witches towards Ilkley Moor. I slammed closed the car door and walked over to where Paul was stood holding a soaked rain hood over his head. The weather, was once more, appalling. We were both soaked to the skin, thunder rumbled in the distance, and the map began to disintegrate in our hands. About a hundred yards from the summit of Sword Point, Paul called back to me,

"This is fantastic, the view goes on and on."

At the top, I could clearly see for myself why Paul was so excited. Even though the storm clouds threatened to spoil things for us, the sight that met my eyes , possibly some ten miles distance, depicted a panorama of yellows and browns. The natural essence of Ilkley Moor.

Yes, we were wet and cold, and my thoughts were blurred by the howling winds, but there was a great sense of satisfaction about our discovery. Others in the past, some called them witches, had realized this connection between Sword Point and Ilkley Moor and maybe they had been, like myself, compelled to travel the life quest in their search for the truth. Mainly due to the immense amount of data which shows the Ilkley Moor region to be a focus of highly strange phenomena, I always felt that there was some underlying reason for this. It almost seemed to me at times that something hidden, something with an intelligence, was trying to lure us there, and to assist us in locating that which remained secreted from us. There are cases of people today, who claim that whilst walking those lonely moors, they find through a strange experience (usually associated with ball of lights encounters) themselves being led to certain ancient sites. The same places on the moor keep cropping up in these accounts, as if there is some kind of magical lure.

I believe that those who have come close to this quest in the past, have themselves laid down clues in the landscape for others to find at a later date. Some may have hidden away there knowledge of this secret behind symbolism and dragon crests.

Let us suppose that there is a sword of kinds secreted in the lands of the dragon, a real physical artifact - a sword that is 'different' and holds an importance to those who seek it. In the 17th Century, there were two separate accounts that 'witches' paraded to Ilkley Moor for some important reason. The Timble witches flew in their minds along energy tracks and mapped out their course in written records, whilst the witches from nearby Lancashire, traveled in a more conventional manner by foot from Pendle Hill. Both covens make clear their purpose, their goal a sacred site on Ilkley Moor. In more recent times, during the 19th Century, Freemasons from Keighley sought out an area called the Ashlar Chair (a rectangular piece of open land on the high-top of the moor above Bingley, not

79

far away from the Twelve Apostles stone circle.) and meetings by these masons gave rise to the region being known as *'Rommuls Law'*. A more intriguing account involves occultists from Keighley, based at Parkwood Street, who were an offshoot of the Golden Dawn and reflected their own findings in the *Lamp of Thoth* - a privately published newsletter. Amongst their membership was one of the Lund family. Within their writings, we find that they seemed to be obsessed with visits to the ancient sites on Ilkley Moor, and they make it clear that they were seeking something hidden. Thoth was an ancient Egyptian god of learning and wisdom, who was later remembered in the form of Hermes, the messenger and giver of hidden knowledge. Were they using such occult practices to involve Thoth in their moorland quest?

As I drove the car back towards Otley, Paul's final words of the day echoed in my thoughts, imprinting themselves there for all time, *"You know, it says here in this book that there's an old hall at the foot of Sword Point called Scow Hall. There's something strange on the staircase there; it's like an Egyptian symbol or something – a round, red colored disk. Nobody knows who put it there, or when, but I think it's some kind of magical symbol"*

Driving away from Sword Point, the Sun began to rise overhead and in the distance Ilkley Moor shone under its dazzling brightness.

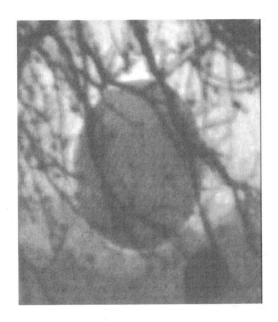

OBOL, Appletreewick. 1983.

CHAPTER THREE

ATEN'S TRUTH

The Orange Ball of Light UFOs, as we have already seen, symbolises significantly the phenomena observed around the Ilkley Moor area. The OBOLs seem to be a trigger, and certainly were responsible for my own involvement within the sword of truth quest. We can also suggest that these OBOLs are closely linked to the ancient megalithic sites found on the moor, and at other more recent historic places of worship like churches, which have been built upon these original ancient sites. But, just what are these OBOLs? Well, there is an intelligence of sorts associated with them, that witnesses often report as being like something that is living or alive. They have the ability to effect the observer/ experiencer in a way that is measured in emotional change, and leave them without full recall of the sighting of the OBOL or what has occurred during the experience.

All of these attributes of the OBOL have been reported many times all over the world, and it has been stated more than once that the overall experience is not only awe inspiring, but quite humbling at the same time. The Rosicrucian, the Illuminati, and other theosophical societies, have regarded the OBOL type phenomena, describing them as maybe angels and other celestial creatures; once again giving these UFOs' a sense of living beings in their own right. According to the Rosicrucian order, they resembled small suns, being creatures of pure energy. This radiant ball was surrounded by streamers of Vril energy force, enhancing the belief that angels had wings. These wings are corona-like fans of light by which these creatures propel themselves through the subtle essences of the super-psychical worlds. No need then, for any clumsy solid flying saucers here it would seem.

Above: The author's wife Helen stands at the site of the Twelve Apostles Stone Circle.

In November, 1982, Steve Hart was on his way home from my house at that time in Addingham, and whilst he sat traveling on the bus he noticed a bright ball of orange light that was moving over the adjacent moorland. As he continued to look at it, an overwhelming feeling of dread and sorrow overcame him and yet, he could not think why this should be happening to him. He began to question his own thoughts and ability to reason this, but then when he arrived home in Leeds, he returned to the sad news that his grandmother had died, passing away at the same time on that day, when he witnessed the OBOL. An almost identical thing happened to a Morris Dancer in Appletreewick a year later. I was part of the team to investigate this occurrence. This time, the actual OBOL was captured on photographic film, even though nobody reported seeing anything unusual at the time. As in the first case, however, it was later discovered that the brother of the person the OBOL was positioned above, died at the exact time of the photograph being taken.

It was around this time, that I became aware of a run of coincidences connecting my own 1980 OBOL experience, with other stranger encounters from the north of the UK. One of these took place at Todmorden on the Yorkshire & Lancashire borders, within days of my own sighting in November.. Jayne, a middle-aged farmers' wife, lived in the rural countryside just outside the township of Todmorden. Her husband and two sons worked the farm, rearing livestock and growing some cereal crops. The terrain in this area is rough and rugged, open and craggy, with looming hills on all sides, lovely in the summertime, equally harsh in the winter. It was late November, the days were getting longer and duller, making the workload of the farm seemingly heavier and harder as winter approached.

Jayne fell into a deep sleep, slumbering on due to the intense workloads of that day. Then, with a start, she awoke. With her attention unwittingly guided to the bedroom window, she soon noticed a dazzling bright orange light that was entering the room right through the closed window. The time approached 01.00am. She turned over towards her husband in bed at the side of her, but even though she tried to get his attention by pulling at his arm, he remained oblivious to her actions. By now, the light was getting even brighter and began to alarm Jayne, so she got out of bed. Now she found that the light was coming from an orange colored object that was outside of the window. This orange ball hovered in mid air above the end of a field adjacent to the farmyard. She continued to stare at the UFO for ten seconds more, her husband had rolled over in the bed and was now facing the window himself but remaining in his deep sleep. Jayne decided to go outside to have a closer look at the object. Dressed in her nightgown, she was about to reach for the stairs bannister, when, inexplicably, she found herself transported outside without recall of how she had actually got there herself. Sitting on the grass, Jayne was positioned so she looked straight at the OBOL, and it was at this point that she noticed that there were three dark figures standing underneath and next to the illuminating object.

85

As she looked on, Jayne found that there seemed to be a kind of magnetic pull on her body which kept her on the ground. The three ghostly looking humanoids began to move slightly closer in her direction, and Jayne began to cry.

She noted in an instant that they were all wearing similar black coveralls (remember my daughter Sara's encounter at Addingham) with hooded cowls, reminding her of underwater divers. She got the impression that whoever these entities were, 'they' knew her. In the next instant, with another reality-jump, she found herself back in bed, once again trying to alert her husband, but the orange light had disappeared. Was this nothing more than a bad dream? At 06.00 am the couple got up for work, but were disturbed an hour and a half later, when their eldest son came in the farmhouse kitchen for his breakfast. He remarked that over half of the chickens in their stock had been found dead. These fowl had been in the exposed chicken run next to the coup. The mystery deepened when he stated that all of the birds that were under cover, were perfectly unaffected and still living. Jayne knew that the chicken run was positioned exactly where she had observed the OBOL and entities in the early hours of that morning. Surely this was far too big a coincidence? I was further astounded to learn when I visited the farm in early 1990, that less than 25 yards from where Jayne said the OBOL had been positioned, were the remains of an Anglo Saxon burial mound from which ancient relics had been found alongside human remains. Our 'ancient connection' remained intact at this OBOL site.

These are reports of a phenomena that we are still trying to understand today, and it would seem that the origins of these OBOLs lay somewhere in our distant past.

At this point we should return to Ancient Egypt, back thousands of years to the particular sovereign rule of the Pharaoh Akhenaten. The so-called 'heretic king', who's actions changed the course of our world's history as we know it, was in himself an enigmatic personality. In the course of his life, he encountered a phenomenon which we would call today the OBOL, and this effected him to the degree that he built an entire new religion from the experience. His advent onto the throne at Thebes in the 18th Dynasty was sudden, and due to his unusual approach to rulership, taking a path that enforced his reputation as being a 'carer for life', Akhenaten soon fell out of sorts with the established priesthood of Amun-Re, who had built their power in Egypt by the way of fear and oppression. There are important figures from Akhenaten's reign that we need to look at, including Nefertiti; the pharaoh's wife and one of his daughters, Meritaten. They were personalities that enabled a complete change in the world view, and through their lives, it is possible to understand religions as we do so today.

The historic image of Akhenaten portrays a ruler who was

obsessed with the worship of the Aten - the solar disk. We learn that Akhenaten built his own center of rule at Akhetaten (horizon of the Sun disk) - in the middle Egyptian deserts at Armarna, and from there, with his wife Nefertiti and family, proclaimed that there was no other God than the sole deity, the Aten. In truth, history may have been somewhat different, and even the way that the Aten had been realised by Akhenaten might have been interpreted differently, if this occasion had been accounted for, and assessed by Egyptologists, in a more open-minded and profound way. Even the late Cyril Aldred, a well respected scholar of the Armarna period, seemed to be grasping at straws when considering the true reasons for the advent of Aten worship, and the geographical placement of Akhetaten. In his book, Gods of Eden, Andrew Collins writes,

"He pointed out that the gap in the eastern hills above the Royal Wadi, where the sun is seen to rise from the position of the city at certain times of the year, seems to resemble a saddle-back indentation, similar to the hieroglyph used to denote the word akhet, 'horizon'. It was therefore conceivable that Akhenaten may have witnessed the sun emerging between this gap on a visit to the region, and, seeing this as some kind of sign given to him by the Aten, sealed his decision to build a city here and name it Akhetaten, the 'horizon of the Aten'."

Indeed, many of the hieroglyphics from the Armarna

period, do show the Aten as a red-orange solar disk, often with many arms ending in life giving hands, depicted like the rays of the sun, and the orb being positioned between the cleft of two hills. Strangely enough, many modern day observers of the OBOL phenomenon, report seeing such, in remote places, over undulating hillside terrain. It seems very unlikely that this natural occurrence of repeated rising's and setting's of the sun between the cleft of two hills would be enough to convince Akhenaten that the whole basis of religion in Egypt had been previously incorrect and that there were no other gods other than the Aten, or for that matter, there ever had been.

No, something much more profound must have occurred, which would have been important enough to have manifest this new religious conviction in the mind of the Pharaoh Akhenaten had many titles associated to his name including the world's first idealist, the first individual, first prophet of history, with even comparisons being made between his ideas and those of Christ centuries later. His own words and poetry give an idea as to the kind of person we are dealing with here, someone far removed from the typical image we have of an all powerful Egyptian ruler. In his Hymn to the Aten, he writes in his own regal hand, verse that is comparable with the Hebrew Psalms:

"Since thou did establish the Earth,
thou has raised them (men alive) for thy son,
who came forth from thy limbs, the King living in Truth,

Nigel Mortimer

Whilst the whole Earth is in sunlight, I immersed in darkness. "

The author overshadowed by his guide, Akhenaten.

It has been stated recently, that the figure of Moses was probably a later remembrance of Akhenaten's rulership, his ideals and his turn to a monotheistic religion. Indeed, there are many parallels here, even the way that God spoke to Moses on Mt. Sinai from the burning bush according to the Bible, does not seem too far removed from Akhenaten's communion with the OBOL/Aten phenomenon; in both cases there was a transference of rules and commandments from the God-source, outlining the way this new monotheistic religion should emerge. Is there any historical evidence that the figures Akhenaten and Moses are the same or influenced each other? Akhenaten was born about 1394 BC. This correlates with the time that Moses was supposed to have been born at the frontier city of Zarw. Akhenaten's father, Amenhotep III, had married into a mixed race, his queen Tiye being of Israeli descent. Could this be the reason why there are no Egyptian historical records of Akhenaten's youth; in that he had spent much of those early years before his teens without mention and without royal recognition? Writer, Amed Osmans believes that his father may have given orders to the effect that Akhenaten (then Amenhotep IV) be banished from Egypt, effectively ending the chance of a co-regency between the two. Again, this is interesting in view that the biblical story of Moses has the baby, after the Pharaohs threat of murder, being hidden in the bulrushes by the daughter's of the king, then spirited away to safety on the Nile in a basket. It could be speculated that Queen Tiye sent her son Akhenaten, safely away to her home lands under the guardianship of her close relatives at

Goshen. If this was the case, then it could be considered that Akhenaten would have been taught the ways, customs and religions of this foreign land. Maybe he had been influenced by the teachings of their one god, Jehovah -the god of the sky.

Four years after his return to Thebes in 1382 BC, on hearing about the illness of his father, Akhenaten (then aged twelve or thirteen) married Nefertiti. Soon after, he began to build the first Aten temples at Karnak and Luxor, causing so much hostility with the Amun-Re priests that once again Akhenaten was forced out into the deserts half way between Thebes and Cairo. Here we see, yet again, correlations with the Moses story of the bible, in which the central character is sent into exile in the desert wastes.

In 1367 BC, Akhenaten became the sole-ruler of Upper and Lower Egypt. He then shut down many of the temples dedicated to the ancient gods, and through doing so put his life and those of his family at risk. We will see that one of his daughters' born of Nefertiti, decided to flee her ancient homeland in Egypt, which was now in political turmoil, there was plague rife throughout the land, and a time of great natural disasters including earthquakes and volcanic eruptions just north of that great land. With followers of the Aten religion, she set sail along established trading routes, traveling northwards through the Mediterranean, and into the southern reaches of Europe. Their final destination would be in a strange new land, equally hostile, and far removed from the advanced civilisation that she had once known. Her name was Meritaten, but in her new homeland she became known as Scota.

Akhenaten had a motto in his time, *'the king living in truth'*. When I first read those words, something clicked in me, and I felt as if I had heard them somewhere before. There seemed to be a hidden theme running through what I was frequently discovering in my quest to establish what lay behind the origins of the OBOL. My quest for Hakon, had shown me that he wielded a sword of truth, he spent his early life alongside King Athelstan converting the pagans of England to Christianity, and he obtained a right to govern his homeland in a just and honest way. Here, we see a similar pattern emerging. A different time and place in history, but all the same, the central characters being sovereign rulers of their period. Akhenaten, through his own interaction with the OBOL phenomenon which had been known to his Egyptian ancestors as the god-figure Aten, set out to proclaim the truth to his peoples. This was no man-made truth, but one that had its origins beyond human comprehension. It was *'the'* truth -a truth with utter and undeniable certainty, a truth outside of human perceptions.

Nigel Mortimer

Channeling received September, 1991:

'The mists of time spread out in front of the great king's gaze. He beheld the view in front of him, and from his mighty position, high above all that was ordinary, he contemplated that which he had been. Great feelings of sorrowful pity overcame him. Many times, he had tried to look for reason in the way his fellow man often journeyed the negative path of life, and although he had tried himself to take the positive route, inwardly he knew that each had been equally difficult. Over many lifetimes, the great king had been persecuted for following the path of truth, but he knew that no mortal man could change his conviction and it was this inner faith that enabled him to find salvation. He knew that all the greatness surrounding him as King, was worth very little in truth. He was really like everyone else, living the lesson-life, and here to be a leader, yes, but also here to be taught by those below his station. There were others around him, who held positions of power, some were lords and knights, but they abused their positions of man-made privileged.

'He knew, that this man- made power could be easily taken away, it was hollow and fabricated, it was imagery. There was no real sense of reality about these self-made titles -good and bad men alike could hold these positions with equal right.

The king had been fated to lead men in 'his' way, right or

wrong. *It was all that he knew in this lifetime. But inside, he knew that the truth would never change, and by that he would lead men to find this truth within themselves also. He sighed, and gazed once more upon the rolling mists. On the downwardly spiraling path of the negative, so many who he had known had failed to learn, and turn to the way of the truth and the positive realisation. This was the only way to the truth. He remembered that it was not always this way, for he too had once been like them, undecided with no real direction, but a spark within his soul began to evolve like an embryonic cell, reaching out to be recognised with true meaning in his life.*

It was at this time, that the great king began to grow stronger inwardly, transcending to the positive way of life. At the same time, it seemed to the king that there were others, unseen, around him that had been guiding him and evolving this recognition within himself? He began to receive visions and dreams that opened up the way forward, giving him enlightenment, the first steps along the soul-journey to the truth. After he departed the earth, the great king left behind a legacy which would lead other men towards the positive path. He knew that they too, would be assisted by the guardians of the truth, when this help was needed against the specters of negativity. Each would follow his own quest for truth, great or small, and all would eventually find that there was always the one and only truth.

CHAPTER FOUR

THE SWORD OF THE SPIRIT

As I walked up the moorland track that runs alongside the gorge at either side of Backstone Beck on Ilkley Moor, I reflected upon the vision of the great golden sword of truth that I had witnessed hanging over the standing stones of Backstone Circle. I looked back down the moorland slopes, down over the Ilkley township, and my eye caught sunlight glinting off the clock tower of the Parish church. In September, 1991 at a prayer meeting in the church, members of the congregation spent part of an hour together, seeking God's Will for the future. They sought a vision for the way forward, a purpose for the church and its true direction in the coming years. Being utterly unaware of their intentions, I found myself somewhat shaken and amazed to learn in February 1993, of what had in fact, happened after their seeking of Gods guidance through prayer. Curate of the church in 1991, Tony Kidd, saw in his minds-eye, a sword that was emerging through the roof of the nave of the building. Floating down with majestic splendor, the sword embedded itself into the floor of the center isle.

"It came through the roof at an angle, and its tip

disappeared into the ground" the curate later reported, "Sometimes when prayer is offered over such matters a word is given which enables every proposal to be tested against quite precise parameters, 'Does this fit in with our vision for the way forward?'. Indeed the word may become a mission statement (or part of it), in its own right."

The sword was double edged and golden in colour; it was highly polished and seemed to glow with an extremely warm and rich vibrancy. It seemed almost to be alive, so warm was its colour and texture. Tony shared the vision with the meeting at the time and, having received visions of the sword at rest on three subsequent occasions, shared the entire vision during an evening of prayer and fasting in July 1992.

A life sized model of the golden sword seen in the church vision was placed over the knave in 1991.

During the early hours of Tuesday, August 4th 1992 our vicar, Peter Marshall and our Ordained Nick Tucker were each wakened early by feelings that God was speaking to them concerning the vision. Nick felt that the vision is God telling the church in this place (Ilkley) to develop it as a center for spiritual refreshment in our town '*Begin here*' being the key words. The vicar saw the descent of the sword from above, its cross-shaped handle and its arrival in the center of the church as each being of great significance. (An exact model of) the sword was originally placed above the pulpit and it still remains in the church to remind them of the vision and the responsibility to respond to it. It also symbolised very powerfully the power of God's word when spoken under His authority, claimed Peter Marshall. *Jesus said, "I have not come to bring peace, but a sword". Matt.10.34 & "Accept the word of God as the sword which the spirit gives you". Eph.6.17*

So what did we have here? Visions of great golden swords yet again, but this time associated with a Christian Church of early origin in the valley below the pagan sites of Ilkley Moor. We have already seen that the church tower was previously a focus for OBOL sightings and that it was above this very tower that I photographed the face of the Viking leader Hakon. This was all becoming far too much for it to be any coincidence I thought.   In 1900, local Wharfedale author, Harry Speight wrote,

" Whatever may be their (stone circles) relative position in other places, at Ilkley they mostly lay along the moor

98

having an outlook to the east, and if there be any meaning in this, it is interesting to note again how Christian symbolism is based on older custom, for all our churches are made to point to the rising sun; the symbol of the Christian savior, and of his future expectations."

Aside from a natural beauty, there are a number of aspects about the Ilkley area, that seem to point it out as being 'unique' and somewhat special. We have already looked at some of these pointers including the positioning of the Swastika Stone; itself being one of only three carvings of that kind to be found anywhere else in the world, the positioning of more ancient neolithic and Bronze Age sites and rock carvings within a square mile area than anywhere else in Britain, the moor lays at the geographical center of England - the heart of the country, a long history of myths and legends associated with strange Ariel phenomena, records of which date back to Roman times, and even world wide fame derived from the song about a love affair on Ilkley Moor, of which interestingly the words begin, "Where hast tha bin since I saw thee?" (on Ilkla Moor Bhat' at) meaning 'where have you been without your hat on the moors.

Without a shadow of doubt, there is something compelling about the locality. It has even been rumored that Darwin himself, first began to form his world changing Theories about Evolution whilst visiting the healing spas of Ilkley, so inspired was he by the enigma of the place. It has been, and remains a focus for the unusual, and through that recognition, Ilkley and 'the moor' holds secrets that are only just beginning to be understood by modern man.

There is a truth about the real geographical existence of

Ilkley Moor too, which has yet to be revealed. That truth has been emerging slowly, and from time to time, we have been noticing it through record and writings. It is without coincidence that early man should build and position so many stone monuments in this landscape. They were his own statement that the Moor was a unique place, one which he found to be conducive with his own attempts to connect with a phenomenon that was apart from himself and resided in a parallel world unseen. Soon, he would devise a way to commune with this phenomenon, he would locate regions on the Moor, which magnified his ability to receive direction and purpose from the divine, and he would mark these places with the natural materials found there, to create his stone circle temples.

The earliest forms of religion had been born, and Man began to worship at these sacred sites; the forerunners of today's churches. Throughout mankind's history, there have been signs and visions given to those who wish to see, at these ancient places. Where these symbolic inspirations originate, remains for now, unknown, but they offer a chance to understand what has been going on. This has to do with truth and leadership, and it has to do with the way man's destiny is based upon the foundations of his true past. It will be revealed to all of us, that the history of this world is not quite the way it should be.

There are certain occurrences in this mysterious world, that have been changed by those reporting and accounting the events throughout time and which we have all been taught for hundreds of years, to be our true record of the past. These historians have been giving us falsehoods and perversions wherever there had been events in history that didn't fit in with what they would have everyone think was the correct way. In truth, there remains a hidden knowledge that has not been allowed to surface for thousands of years, but from time to time, there have been those who sought to live in truth, and to that aim, reveal not only our true origins, but also the true legacy of mankind.

Just before my OBOL experience in 1980, a number of men and women throughout Britain began to receive remarkable psychic messages that were to eventually bring them all together. In doing so, they set out on their own quest to discover a mysterious green stone which was said to unlock the darkest secrets of the ancient world. These messages were purportedly being received from no other than Akhenaten and also King Arthur's queen Gwenevarr, which at first would seem ridiculous, in that both entities seemed lands apart with no connection whatsoever. In any case, the questors followed the information channeled to them, which eventually led to the actual physical retrieval of a short sword found in the foundations of a footbridge in Worcestershire. This sword led them to the location of the green stone, an ancient gem buried in a heavy brass casket on the banks of the River Avon. At the *place of darkness*' (remember the 'place of horrors' on Ilkley Moor) the Meonia Stone as it came to be known, seemed essential to ridding evil from this land. Since around 4000 BC megalithic man lived in harmony with his natural world, acknowledging life-giving energies obvious to his natural instincts and now lost senses. But then, about 2500 years later, everything changed and his coexistence with the land began to crumble and with it, the knowledge once held by his long forgotten ancestors. The advanced megalithic races moved southward out of Europe towards the African continent, taking with them remnants of the 'hidden' history of early mankind.

'The golden sword hung silently over the stones of the circle : author's own sketch.

In her psychic messages, Gaynor Sunderland, is foretold how this megalithic priesthood not wanting to loose any of the special appreciation of the spirit and its' energies which they harnessed in the great stones that we find today in stone circle formations, secreted themselves into Egypt around 1400 BC, finding Akhenaten's reign and religion, one that was in appreciation of the truth.

They were happy to pass on their knowledge into the safe hands of the peoples of the Aten, but after the kings demise, we have seen how his religion was quickly abandoned by all but a few. In order to escape persecution and plague that was rife in Egypt, under the leadership of

Akhenaten's daughter, Meritaten, the keepers of the first knowledge, found a way out, through the trade routes of central Europe once more. An Egyptian princess walking the shores of her new homeland miles away from the meandering Nile, in no other place than here in the Emerald Isles of Ireland.

CHAPTER FIVE

RETURN OF THE CELESTIALS

Channeling received 20th January 2003 -White Bear Meditation:

'The crown rests on the heads of the children of your world and through them you will understand our reasons for interrelation with you all. We are always here when you call and ready to help. Many are the names you have given us and we answer to all. Distance from you is never an issue, for we will always be at your side. When you were children, your parents were the guardians of your welfare, because you did not understand the world outside of your knowledge at that time in your life. Now, as adults, the knowledge of the world that you exist in is received at a greater pace. We would like you to try to understand that the knowledge that you learn about throughout your lives is only based upon input from reports and other information, often second-hand and never experienced by you, yourself.

The true knowledge which is important to you is found in that which is only gained through your own experiences accepting this knowledge, you will be able to acquire a value which alters not only the physical sense of your reality, but also the very essence of your body which resides in the ether, which you call the spirit.

This knowledge is with you always, throughout all time. If you decide to disregard that which we say, you will still be only moving away from how things will be for you in all eventuality. The whole of your recorded history does not exist in tablets of stone, but can be still found within the hearts of true men who walk with one foot in the spiritual realms. The truth was always there, for all time. You live your lives to experience, and that is how you learn about yourselves. Nobody else can tell you how to live your life. Often, you are willing to receive knowledge from those who themselves have never experienced that which they pronounce. This is an error, for they offer you blind words and not always the truth. There is a point arising soon for all of you to finally understand this. Do not always presume that knowledge is linked to an evolutionary path. Understand that true knowledge of the heart, was even with the simplest of men. In your historic past, you were given chances to accept this understanding of the true knowledge. You understood them as ideas, inventions, scientific, artistic and medical advancements, but at each step of the way, you were capable of corruption, and through this, changed the true essence of the knowledge that you received.

Times ahead will change Man, his environment and his

*expectations, because the human heart can only be filled
to a point with that which is not true. Once all true hearts
and minds can link to become as one in your knowledge,
then a brighter world for all will be so easily achieved. A
new dawn approaches when mankind in spirit will evolve.
We feel now that there are those amongst you who will
accept our teachings -that which we give from the heart.
They will suddenly realise this thirst for the true
knowledge in themselves, so put the books aside, put the
pens down, and begin to seek that which you know to be
right. Your spirit feeds on that which resides in the higher
energies, and through this, you will do wondrous things.*

*We understand that many of you will decide for yourselves
not to follow this path, for your time is not near. We wait
for you with open and embracing hearts. For those that
do, we accept you as our brothers and sisters in this world,
in this lifetime, and in the others before and after it. As
children, you will wear the crown of knowledge, the
knowledge of truth. To you all, please accept the glowing
golden ball, placed above your heads. Some of you will
accept this and feel our communion with you. Rejoice, for
this is sent to you from the Source, healing for all
humanity, sent with our love for all life, for all time.'*

Sharlek

My life was beginning to get back together again after
the divorce from Debs, we remained friends and it didn't

seem too bad in that she was happy to let me have regular contact with Lee and Warren. I began to take on guided walks around the ancient sites of Ilkley Moor, and spent many hours there in the kind of work that I enjoyed. The moor was always a friend to me, not just a natural formation, but somewhere that seemed like home. I was never alone whilst I could walk its heather clad slopes, climb its bracken laden crags, and embrace its long-past sense of ancientness at Backstones, the Twelve Apostles, White Wells and beyond. I had made good friends in Jan and Jon Hurst, a couple from Ilkley, who I found to be very connected to spirit and their own set of Celestials. Jon was like a brother to me, I trusted him, knowing that we shared a common sense of awareness of spirit, and Jan, who I had known since the late 90's, was a channel of UFO denizens and spiritual healer. Together, we were much more than friends, we were like a family and it seemed that we had always known each other. Jon has a great spirit about him. He had endured some ill health over the years, and life has been something of a struggle at times, but he always comes battling through. He has a great awareness of things that most people never seem to fully appreciate. I admire that so much in him. People like Jon, are the kind that I put my trust in, so it wasn't too surprising to find I could talk to him about all the things I hid from those who didn't understand 'what I was about', and he saw in me my passion to find out the truth. He 'knows' me, I am certain of that, if nothing else.

Nigel Mortimer

It was the year of my fortieth birthday, 1999. The new millennium was just around the corner, bringing with it a renewed interest in all things new age and supernatural. There had been an increase in UFO activity around the Wharfedale region, and I was now concentrating my efforts on investigating reports from Ilkley Moor once again. Jon knew of the messages that I had been receiving in the way of life-lessons from the soul incarnate Akhenaten, and he was eager to see if it would be possible for me to channel (receiving psychic information in a trance like state) the kind of UFO entities that he and Jan had been in contact with for several years previous. This seemed to be a natural development of how things had been going along in the sword quest, and his suggestion wasn't entirely new to me for I had felt that since my experience with Helju and her transmogrification, these kind of other-worldly entities, although unseen, had been around me in my day to day life for quite some time.

All along the way, it was as if I was being maneuvered, even in little things that seemed to happen by chance. For example, in June 2002, I was out walking by Backstones Circle, when I glanced down at the side of the track I was on. There, hidden at the foot of a clump of bracken next to one of the upright standing stones of the circle, I found a folded piece of A4 paper. Upon opening it I found the following narration along with a series of strange symbols written in black ink pen:

The Circle & The Sword

'Peace, Love and light to the reincarnation platform during the chaos time. Fight evil within and without and the Atlantean soul group will reach the 7th dimension known as Stargate. Let every human soul in body and spirit be returned to their original path of light and love and bring justice to those who were wrongly accused and abused by the evil ones from M.......... Help all those souls currently trapped and off their path so they can be reunited to their higher self in Stargate. Allow the light to enter the earth-plane by the white light workers of power, truth and justice. Allow it to flow in the direction of Sun (Ra), clockwise in motion so the grid is taken, let every soul be empowered with new strength and courage during these dangerous times. End of Stargate transmission. The grail, the sword, the rainbow and the white horse of spiritual freedom.'

Rantings of an over-imaginative mind? Maybe, but if so, how do we account for certain elements within this text that point to what I was already aware of within the sword quest and the awakening of Backstone Circle over a decade before. The originator remains unknown, but whoever it was, seems to have known certain things about the location where they had decided to secret this 'transmission' to Stargate.

There seems to be an equality in the amount of fine and wet days throughout the year around Ilkley Moor, and this day was one of the later. It had been drizzling rain most of the morning, but Jon and I had decided that in the evening we would venture the moors once more. Something had been building up between us both, that same old inner feeling that we had to 'follow' the urgency that came out of nowhere, but compelled one to see where it would lead to. I don't remember many words between the two of us that day, just a sense of knowing, even to the degree that we knew where we would end up on the moor, and that when we eventually did reach this destination, it would be for some important reason. To those that know of its' whereabouts, 'the hole' (as I affectionately call it) on Ilkley Moor, is probably the single most important location site to be found anywhere in the course of the sword quest. There is very good reason for me making that claim, which will become clearer in due course.

The site is literally a massive hole or hollow that looks to have been scooped out of the moorland landscape. No one quite knows how it was formed, and there are explanations from it being the remnants of a world war two bomb hole, to a crater left by an impacting meteor. Whatever, there is evidence that within the 'hole' itself are the remains of an ancient iron aged bell pit and megalithic stone formations. The site lays claim to fame in the ufological sense too, as it is the actual location for the Ilkley Moor Alien abduction and photographic case of December 1st, 1987. This single case, still unexplained, is probably the best evidence we have for UFO reality here in the UK, if not also anywhere else in the world!. Funny, that it should have happened right here on Ilkley Moor, just where 'Sword Point' points to.

As Jon and I walked along the high sided track way running into the hole, that gives the impression that one is leaving this world and seemingly entering another, I couldn't help but reflect upon the 'chance' that may have been offered to Hakon. Should we have been following in his Viking footsteps, those that he once strode, wielding Quernbiter, and facing the unknown truths of this supernatural gateway into the unknown. I wondered silently, I listened, and I looked around in amazement at this natural amphitheater, and as I did so, it seemed as if a vortex of unseen energies swirled in the essence of a long forgotten time. Spinning. Spinning.....spiral's of energies.

Darkness had fallen, but a tranquility filled the arena, dispelling all feelings of fear. Jon and I casually chatted and continued to wonder what was in store for us there. Why had we been led to this place, for what purpose? I raised my head towards Jon and without a single moment of hesitation uttered words that for seconds made no sense to either of us, yet I could do nothing to cease this flow of prose from my mouth, *"The rains shall fall...., The rains shall fall...."*

An inner voice in my head, something that I recognised, yet not any part of my self, dictated that simply the heavens shall open and down will surely come the rains. Quite prophetic? I don't think so, but that is just what did happen. The rains did fall. No sooner had I spoken these words, there came a change in the atmosphere within the hole that could not be readily explained. Then the blackened skies opened and drenched the two of us in a resplendent downpour. Soaked to our skins in seconds, Jon and I stood there looking at each other. The sudden prophecy had been fulfilled. Or, had it? As the rain continued to pour its cleansing qualities upon us, I felt compelled to close my eyes and simply receive that which had begun to take place. Almost as soon as I did, there formed within the face of something that I can only describe as glorious. Features of a head enshrouded in a golden vibrancy appeared out of the depths of that place uncharted somewhere between the realms of our minds and soul. I knew this face. It looked almost human, not quite. Here was something above humanity, angelic and filled with the compassion of everything good and decent in the universe. I don't know how, but I knew his name, his title, his 'tag'. I was in the presence of the Celestial, Sharlek.

In that moment with Jon at the hole on Ilkley Moor, my life changed once again. From then on I began to know the things that I had searched for over years. I had reached a point of acknowledgment, I was being given the keys to the door, I was being given the right to hold aloft the sword of truth, and I had the distinct feeling that I could throw away my L-plates. I had passed the test of years. Something I had lost back in 1980, when all of this first started, had been returned to me in the moments that Sharlek revealed his presence and drew close to me. He returned a heart that had been borrowed in time, and in doing so, gave me the ability to listen with this new found heart.

Now, I would be forever connected to those who have existed alongside humanity since the beginning, and that made me recognize how humble we really are, how the human ego is such a small part in all of this. We connect in spirit, and that is what we all are. In spirit, Sharlek, the Celestials and every one of us human beings, are all connected as One.

The Celestials are no New Age invention. They have been with us, yet separate from us, for thousands of our earth years, and they existed long before the creation of this world. Man has sometimes known these celestial beings, and has called them Angels, but the truth is we are all Angels in one form or another, we are all Beings of Light. They have been here, guiding us through our history. They are healers of the truth and have watched over us, as we have corrupted the truth of our very own existence. Time and again, our misguided forefathers misreported events in our historic past, in order to gain, whether that be for political power or just through force of

113

the ego. The Celestials know that our greatest challenge is that of facing our own truth. Without that, we will never really know who we are, who we were, and who we will become. Sharlek informed me through a process we call channeling (in my case a trance-like state, in which I allow the presence of the celestial being to enter my physical body and use my senses to project a message or transfer universal healing energies) that he was with humanity in the physical form during the times of the Atlantean era. At that time many human and Celestial friendships had been formed, and through our mutual work in healing, Sharlek and I bonded. It would not be untrue to say that he and me are the same, but this should not lead one to conclude that Sharlek is no more than my delusion. I think the evidence offered here, is testimony to the emergence of Sharlek as a wholly separate entity to myself. It is through his prophecy that I continue to work alongside him, and in doing so, I am given back evidence of his reality. He has interacted with those human personages in our past, that I have rediscovered since the OBOL experience in 1980; Akhenaten, Hakon, and others, all existing as soul aspects of the same divinity, and all with the intent in their lives to seek out the truth about who we are, and just where we might be heading?

The Celestial beings, of which Sharlek is a part, and indeed we all are, follow the actions of those who work towards the truth. This can be to seek out the truth in many areas, large or small, it doesn't really matter. The only thing that does, is the ability to recognise it, and in doing so, begin to accept that we are all the same and respect that notion. We are all beings of light, no matter where we originate; whichever country here on Earth, whichever planet or star system, indeed anywhere in dimensional space or time. This can only be born out of intention. The right intention, moralistically, and in honesty with oneself.

There was a time in our recent history, around the time of Akhenaten, when certain keepers of the truth attempted to change human viewpoints to the fact that there is, in truth, only one single force of creation which we call God. There are aspects of God, there are Angelic Beings, and there are Human Beings, and various other life-forms; all of whom are progressing towards the truth and some of these, from time to time, are helped along their way by those who, as we would say, *'are nearer to God'*, meaning that they have progressed spiritually towards a better understanding of the truth. One of these was the daughter of Akhenaten, forced out of her homeland in Egypt to eventually arrive on the shores of southwestern Ireland.

Nigel Mortimer

Drawing by Jon Hurst - his depiction of the author Nigel Mortimer when channeling.

Daughter Of The Light

Channeled from Sharlek: 14th January, 2004

The year 2004, is going to be very significant, for it heralds a new beginning. It is the start of the era of the 7th Sun -a historical timescale laid down by the Atlantean Light Healers for mankind's evolutionary and more importantly, spiritual path. It will be a year of revelations. All who seek, will see with new eyes. All who listen, will hear with open hearts and All who accept the true purpose of their being, will find their true Self. Thousands of years ago, the 'carriers of the first knowledge', (themselves descendants of the Light Healers) - explorers from the eastern lands- visited the shores of what we call today the British Isles.

At that time the original races of this land were split into various isolated farming communities and groups with fragmented leadership. In your history, you call that period the Bronze Age. Your ancestors lived meager lives in constant combat with the elemental forces, and out of this grew the seeds of religious worship, albeit in a very simplistic form. Around 1560BC, the ancients of the eastern lands, in particular Egypt, began to expand trading routes with other localised countries, but northern Europe still lay in the most, an uncharted region. While the pre-ancient Egyptians had been building giant pyramids and sophisticated burial tombs, the early peoples of Britain were intellectually still emerging from the stone age, yet retained within themselves a spiritual awareness from an even earlier epoch, for we knew of their first peoples and many of them worked alongside our kind in the healing temples of the lands you call Atlantis.

When the travelers of the eastern lands arrived on the shores of the British Isles, bringing with them the knowledge of the truth, those native to the land who were spiritually awakened, greeted the newcomers and welcomed them into their clans. There were others who did not take on board this new learning, and remained in

117

the darkness, continuing to follow their old ways and pagan worship. In time, however, even they began to see the importance of the knowledge that had been lost to humanity from the first time, and it was these people who sought to replicate the religion that the travelers brought with them to this new found land.

One of these travelers was the daughter of the Pharaoh Akhenaten, she was wise and had been touched, like her father, by the wisdom of the Aten. We worked closely with Meritaten and her followers because we could see that she was a daughter of the light, and in her heart she carried the truth, and she wished to serve mankind with this knowledge without any gain for herself, even in those difficult and dark times in your history. She could see that the natives of this land were spiritually aware because they had been genetically linked to the first time, and their descendants were of the Atlantean races, but had lost the ability to appreciate the knowledge she carried. With her followers, she roamed the lands of the Celts, and it was through her information, that they built the megalithic monuments that we find across these northern Isles today. Meritaten became a great leader due to her wisdom and sense of the truth, and the peoples of this new found land called her Scota, the founder of the Scottish races. There had already been a cult of Sun worship here, before Meritaten arrived, and after her death on the British shores, the natives continued to develop their own appreciation of this new religion, alongside the knowledge that she had left behind. Their stone monuments and stone circles were attempts to build in a manner that would match the obelisks and great oracle temples of the Aten, back in the ancient Egyptian lands.

Without fully understanding, they built at places where they had themselves, found communion with our kind and the forces of the One. They laid stones in a circular fashion to emulate their contact with the Aten, which in truth was at many times, our presence, being made available to them in the hope that they would find a way towards the truth and the light. This is the importance of the ancient sites that you find today all over Europe and the northern lands. They are replications of the temples and places of communion that we created in the first epoch. At these places, some of which are desolate and in ruin today, we can draw close to you, but more importantly, you can learn to draw close to our kind too. Scota, in her time, knew that it would be beneficial to the followers of the light, for her to lay down and secrete items that she carried with her from the descendants of the Atlanteans. These included some of her own personal items, which carried the energies of the Pharaoh, and amongst others were the precious stones and crystals of healing. The stone circle sites are the Key to unlocking your futures.

Reaching this point in the channeling, Sharlek went on to

reveal his prophecy to me, concerning the actual whereabouts of one particular hidden item once carried by Scota (Meritaten), and how it could be located today,

With good reason, we are fast approaching the time when mankind will become aware once more of the true path of his history, and it will be through these 'discoveries' of out of the place items and artifacts, which will provide undeniable proof of it. As I write this at the start of 2004, I now know where and when the discovery of a single shebu collar, the kind depicted around the necks of the King and his family during the Armarna period in Egypt (which was in the possession of Scota/Meritaten up until shortly before her death on British shores) will be made.

 This information, channeled to me by Sharlek in late 2003, gave instruction to travel within the UK to the actual site of this buried collar, locate it by remote viewing, which would in effect 'activate' the procedure for another party of people to locate, dig for and retrieve the artifact.

Obviously, a find of a physical object pertaining to origins in Ancient Egypt, being found at a place called Glenscota, meaning the Glen of Scota, in southern Ireland, would be enough to turn the history books upside down, yet I can do no less than take that which Sharlek has revealed to me, as fact and in truth, and it is my intention to act upon his will in the hope that soon Sharleks' truth and that of the Celestials will be common place amongst the peoples of this world. When I look back at the incredible journey I have lived through in my adult life and reflect upon it, I think about the many twists and turns that to most would seem impossible. I wouldn't blame anyone to read the pages of my life, and think to themselves this must be all made up, it's far too fantastic to be real, and this guy must be deluded. But, as I hope I have shown, there were always others there, witnesses to my journey and the events that took place along it. I seem to have lost more than most in my material life, including the trappings of our modern civilisation. Through an over-moralistic attitude and the pressures born of that, my marriages to women that I truly loved in their time, failed miserably. Life was hard without real reason, stealing away all that meant so much to me. Even so, it seemed the higher-purpose was the most important thing keeping me together when all else around me crumbled into dust. Something gave me the will to carry on, and something gave me the strength to leave behind that which was so dear to me. They were people who came and went away in their own time, they all knew me at various times during the past 30 years or so, and they are testimony to the facts contained herein, so for that I am forever grateful.

My association and friendship with Sharlek and other Celestials that I have come to know well in recent years, has grown ever stronger. His channeled messages have been given to many who were prepared to listen with an open heart, and some have even acknowledged his presence themselves while these channeling's were taking place. Wow, he's even appeared on satellite TV in 2002, and that must be a first for any of the old Atlanteans! Through Sharlek I was made aware that the Celestials use these channeling sessions in order to impart universal healing energies to anyone who needs them. And, they know, believe me, who needs them and the reasons why. Sharlek states that for any of us to want to offer healing to any other living being, at any level, is the most precious thing that we can do for each other. This is a universal rule, all who heal and offer themselves as healing vessels are working in the light of God, and that is the closest that we can achieve in the physical to be at one with the source. Compassion for our brothers and sisters elevates us to the level of angels, and is the requirement that the Celestials themselves continue to develop in their own on-going spiritual advancement. They have been developing spiritually for millennium, yet they say that time is an insignificant factor for them in the scale of things. The last twenty four years have been for me, a journey of revelations, psychic experiences, closer contact and proof. I now channel an entity that I know to be an Angelic Celestial and together we are working to heal this planet and all living forms on it, in it and even inside it.

Working mainly on Ilkley Moor where interaction at ancient sites allows such celestial beings to manifest in our world, I continue to contact Sharlek with an open heart and an inquiring mind. I am searching still for the truth and I know that I am not alone in this search. For Sharlek, who's message for Mankind is one of Truth, Wisdom and Light for all, bringing powerful healing energies and insight to anyone who asks, yet he walks a path unseen alongside of me. He is awaiting the time which will soon be upon us all. When this time arrives, as it surely will, we will all know those who for now exist just outside of our physical reach, ever ready to offer themselves as equals and the guardians of our truth. Without prejudice, we should be prepared to reach out to the Celestials, draw them in close to our hearts, and then learn to accept a future in which all Beings of Light, whoever they are, exist as one in the Truth.

God's love and light to all.

Nigel Mortimer

How to channel Sharlek & Other Celestial Guides

Please find time to meditate on the following:

Listen to your heart
It calls to you day to day
Binds universal love within your soul
Where it takes you no other knows
They seek, they search
Listen to your heart and
I will find you there.
Listen to your dreams
They're with you night by night
The keys to the universe all around
Where you go no one knows
Keep seeking, keep searching
Listen to your dreams and I will find you there.
Should our worlds collide at night and all love is lost
Listen to your heart
A new world, united as one, for all.
Listen to your life
It takes you onwards hour by hour
Past, present and future times
Where it ends who can know
Silence holds the answer,
Listen to your life
And I will find you there.

Channeled from Sharlek , 12th January, 2004.

124

UPDATE: MARCH 2011.

It has been over a decade since I wrote this book and in that time I have been searching to find answers which may help quantify the prophecies outlined so far. I suppose one the most intriguing of these concerns the supposed discoveries of ancient artifacts found close to the shores of England at Dogger Bank, where divers have found what looked like the remains of ancient temple foundations mapped out, not unlike buildings we find in coastal areas of the Mediterranean.

Around this time, (summer 2010), psychic Uri Geller hit the mainstream news headlines when he decided to buy what seemed today and insignificant island on the east coast of Scotland. Uri Geller explained that he had been prompted to buy Lamb Island soon after a visit he had to Rosslyn Chapel on the borders in Scotland. Whilst there, he noticed how he could project an imaginary line through significant ancient sites, from Roslin to Lamb Island. Also, he noticed how the group of islands of which Lamb was a part reminded him of the formation of pyramids at the Giza plateau. He declared that it was his intention to survey and investigate the island in the hope that he would be able to locate lost artifacts which may have originated in ancient Egypt. He goes on to mention, that it was whilst reading about the legendary tales of Scota and the foundation of the Scottish race, that he felt the true connection between this ancient Egyptian princess from the Armarna period and her presence in Scotland. Strangely enough, it was while I was also visiting Rosslyn Chapel in 2009, that I became aware of the significance between Scota and the region. In the week prior to my visit, I woke up one morning to find what looked like a small bruise, shaped like a trident or a bird's foot. The mark was clearly there under the skin of my left foot, and remained there for a whole day before disappearing at night. Whilst I was at Rosslyn Chapel, (famous for the Da Vinci Code film). I looked down at the stone steps which lead down into a small anteroom. Amazingly, I could see the same symbol carved into the step, which had appeared as the bruise on my foot. It was even the exact same size.

Later, I was to learn that this symbol was known to ancient Nordic tribes and is often depicted in runes stone symbolism, as a sign of protection. After seeing this in the Chapel, I made myself more aware of the environment around me and tried to take in as much as possible, just in case there might be clues as to why the symbol should be found there. I moved to look at paintings which now surround the upper gallery of Rosslyn Chapel, mostly depicting scenes of the locality and previous owners of the Roslin estates. It was without doubt that the Chapel had a strong and long connection with Scottish Freemasonry and possibly with roots in the Knights Templars, its symbolism to be seen everywhere. Looking at one particular oil painting which showed a scene of the nearby wooded valley of the River Esk, (found just north of the chapel) I suddenly saw two linear streaks of light pass over the frame of the painting, as if some unseen hand had drawn out for me an area I should look at in the picture itself. This flash of light happened twice, each time highlighting this part of the Esk woodland. I looked at a map of the region, and could see that these 'lines' passed close to a significant area in those woods, to the very place where English soldiers had met there deaths in hundreds when pursuing the Scottish hero William Wallace (Braveheart) by going over the sheer cliffs and down into the basin of the flowing Esk waters, not knowing the terrain awaiting them by night in this densely wooded trap set down by Wallace and his followers in their fight against the English invaders. Quite difficult to get to, but not impossible, is Wallaces Cave – found on these cliffs, supposedly his hideout.

The 'lines' continued on in a north easterly direction, out across the borders landscape, until reaching the shorelines of the Firth of Forth, and onwards towards what looks to most people, an insignificant small island of Lamb. Uri Geller wrote in 2010, *'I have been dowsing all my adult life, and I have never experienced such a powerful network of ley lines. It's so strong that there's no doubt in my mind that I have been guided to Lamb by a higher intelligence. Perhaps I will discover that I too have Scottish blood in me.'*

I have no doubts that Uri Geller is on the right tracks here, and it is by little coincidence that he should be the one to acquire Lamb island with all its obvious connections with the pyramids of Giza, ancient Egypt and Scota's ancestors. Uri Geller feels that he may find treasure on the island Again, this connects with Scota in some way and I was so intrigued, I decided to contact Uri Geller in the summer of 2009 to discuss his intentions for the island and to let him know about Sharlek's prediction that evidence would be found by someone other than myself in a prediction made a decade before in the Glen of Scota in Ireland.

Like Ireland, Scotland is also known for its beautiful Glens. The question remains, is the Isle of Lamb the 'glen' of Scota, and if so, did her ancestors leave positive evidence to show that her presence in her own time (and other times too), that can be found there and what could this evidence be, maybe a treasure or maybe something much more significant, maybe a truth?

Twenty four years ago the author underwent a strange UFO experience with an inexplicable ball of light near to Ilkley Moor in Yorkshire. Since then, he has lived a life of psychic experiences, closer contact, and undeniable proof that we are not alone. This is his journey, his true story and the revelation that since the dawn of time, Beings of Light have been watching over Humanity. The Circle & The Sword is a message for all mankind written within the pages of this book.

It is the truth of our past and it is the hope for our future. *We are not alone.*

Sword Vision at Backstones in pen -copyright N.Mortimer.

Bibliography

Spheres Of Influence Nigel Mortimer Addingham 1983
The Call Of Backstones Nigel Mortimer Ilkley, 1999
Daemonologia Grainge, 1882Ilkley Ancient & Modern,
Collyer & turner, 1885
Oedipus & Akhenaten, Vieliosky Abacus Books
The Anglo Saxons, Sir F. Stenton
The Viking Achievement, Foote & Wilson
Pi in the sky, M.Poynder, 1991Upper Wharfedale,
H.Speight
Return to Backstone Circle, Paul Bennett, 1989
The Green Stone, Phillips & Keatman, Granada 1984
Looking for the Aliens, Jenny Randles & Peter Hough
The Ghost Book, McGregor, Hale 1955
Initiation by the Nile, Mona Rolfe, Neville Spearman
Quicksilver Heritage, Paul Screeton, 1974
The Pennine UFO Mystery, Jenny Randles, 1983
The Eye of Fire, Phillips & Keatman, 1986
The UFO Debate, David Barclay 1989
The Dragon & The Disk, F.W. HalidayWharfe Valley
Times, article- July, 1989
EARTH, Paul Bennett, 1983
UFO Brigantia - IUN 1990 & 1989
Flying Saucers Have Landed, Adamski & Leslie
White Bear Channellings - Cath Pimlett,
2002Akhenaten, King of Egypt, Cyril Aldred, 1999
Kingdom of the Ark, Lorraine Evans, 2000
Act of God, Phillips, 1998
The Bible - Revised Standard VersionUri Geller –
Website 2010.

Gods Of Eden, Andrew Collins, 1998
Ghosts & Legends of Yorkshire – Andy Roberts, 1992
Stories of Old Renound – Blackie, 1941
UFO Precedents – N.Mortimer, 1990
Mythology of the British Isles – Geoffrey Ash
The Sword of the Spirit Ilkley Parish Church, 1991
Strange Creatures from Time and Space – John
KeelAlien Contact – Jenny Randles & Paul Whetnall
N.Spearman,1981
Communion – Whitley Strieber, Century 1987
Transformation – Whitley Strieber, Century 1988The
Haunted Moor – Nicholas Size, Ilkley 1934
The Lands Of The Dragon - D. Murgatroyd 1981

Photographic Permissions:
Page 29: William Butterfield inside White Wells
sourceIlkley Gazette – 1898.
Page 41: Copyright Garry Hubert: 2008
Page 98: Copyright Jonathan Hurst: 2001
All other photographic images, sketches and maps
copyright remains with Nigel Mortimer.

Cover Image: N.Mortimer 2014

ABOUT THE AUTHOR

NIGEL MORTIMER
was born in Munster,
Gemany in 1959, returning
to live in his family's
hometown of Otley in
West Yorkshire after
several years in Singapore.
He grew up in
Nottingham and moved
back to Yorkshire in the
late 1970's. He has been
interested in and
experiencing strange
phenomena all of his life.

Biography:
'I have been actively involved in UFO investigations since
1980, after I experienced at first hand a UFO sighting
from my home at that time. I soon became a regional
UFO investigator and researcher for the Northern UFO
Network, run at that time by Jenny Randles (who has used
my work in her books), eventually becoming the Director
of Regional Investigations for BUFORA in the early
1990's. I was the founder of the WYUFORG (West
Yorkshire UFO Research Group) which later became the
IUN (Independent UFO Network).
With other members of the WYUFORG, we were
responsible for solving the Cracoe Fell UFO photographic
case of 1983, which has since gone down in British UFO

lore as one of the best investigated cases, even though the object in question was identified as a natural phenomenon.

I have written articles for many newspapers including the Yorkshire Post, Bradford Telegraph & Argus, and locally the Ilkley Gazette and have had my work included on national and international TV and in Radio programs. I was editor for my own in-house newsletters 'UFO Reporter' and UFO Visitors, plus have written articles for inclusion in major news stand magazines.

My work has been included in a number of UFO books by leading authors, and I was a consultant for the 'If you go down to the woods' chapter in Jenny Randles' Pennine UFO Mystery (Granada).

To date, I have written several published booklets including - ' The UFO Mysteries Of Ilkley Moor', and 'The Circle & The Sword' , updated in 2012 - which describes personal investigations in the Ilkley Moor region and includes previously unpublished material. Since 1990, I have been in 'contact' with Other Worldly Beings, establishing through psychic means an on-going communication with the Celestial known as Sharlek, who I have written about here in 'The Circle & The Sword'.

Own Publications:

1981 – Spheres Of Influence (Dowsing and the Paranormal)

1983-1986 WYUFORG Newsletter (later became UFO Brigantia)

1994 – 1996 UFO Reporter Newsletter. (became UFO Visitors)

1996 – Return Of The Flying Saucerers (Bradford UFO Flap)

1996 – The Call Of Backstones (Addingham UFO

Nigel Mortimer

Entities/Stone Circle)
2001 and 2008 update – UFO Mysteries Of Ilkley Moor
TV shows: (between 1990 -2006)
Edit 5 (Yorkshire TV)
Calendar News (Yorkshire TV)
Good Morning (Granada)
Schofield's Quest (ITV)
The Heaven & Earth Show with Toyah Wilcox
Sky Documentaries (various)
The Scream Team (Living TV)
The Sunday Show (Granada)
BBC & ITV Regional News (various)
Radio:
BBC Radio Leeds
Radio Aire
Pennine Radio
Fresh Radio
Now That's Weird (Ross Hemsworth)
Magazines:
UFO Universe
UFO Times (BUFORA)
UFO Encounters (Uri Geller's)
Encounters
Fortean Times
Sightings Magazine
Nexus Magazine
Current qualifications:
I currently host my own website which debates the
UFO phenomenon, openly and without prejudice, in the
search for the truth and disclosure. It is my personal belief
that not all UFOs are not physical aerial objects from other
planets, but may be projections from a phenomenon

which is truly 'alien' to our current human understanding, but I do believe that this phenomenon has been interacting with humanity for ages past.

I am actively investigating and writing up reports from the Yorkshire Dales, focusing my attention on the Menwith Hill base and its' connection with Ancient sites and light-form phenomena. I speak at UFO Conferences around the UK on a regular basis, and continue to work closely with the media. Until recently, I was employed full time as a tutor working with students suffering learning difficulties; teaching basic skills within a college in Keighley, West Yorkshire, UK, . I now run a book-selling business (specialising in the paranormal) with my wife Helen, from our home in North Yorkshire.

Nigel Mortimer

Also available from Nigel Mortimer

Wisdom Books

AMAZON.COM

32366945R10083

Made in the USA
Charleston, SC
16 August 2014